Revised Edition

under-
resourced
learners

8 strategies to boost
student achievement

Under-Resourced Learners: 8 Strategies to Boost Student
Achievement. Revised Edition.
   Ruby K. Payne
      220 pages
      Bibliography pages 201–208

aha! Process, Inc.
P.O. Box 727
Highlands, TX 77562-0727
(800) 424-9484 ■ (281) 426-5300
Fax: (281) 426-5600
Website: www.ahaprocess.com

Copy editing by Dan Shenk and Jesse Conrad
Book design by Paula Nicolella
Cover design by Dunn+Associates

Printed in the United States of America

ISBN: 978-1-938248-89-4

Library of Congress Control Number: 2008920184

1. Education   2. Sociology   3. Title

Revised Edition

under·resourced learners

8 strategies to boost student achievement

RUBY K. PAYNE, Ph.D.

Other Selected Titles by Ruby K. Payne, Ph.D.

A Framework for Understanding Poverty: A Cognitive Approach

*Research-Based Strategies: Narrowing the Achievement Gap
for Under-Resourced Learners*

How Much of Yourself Do You Own?
(Payne & O'Neill-Baker)

Bridges to Health and Healthcare
(Dreussi-Smith, Payne, Shaw, Young)

From Understanding Poverty to Developing Human Capacity

Working with Parents: Building Relationships for Student Success

*Working with Students: Discipline Strategies
for the 21st-Century Classroom*

*Crossing the Tracks for Love: What to Do When You and Your
Partner Grew Up in Different Worlds*

*Removing the Mask: How to Identify and Develop Giftedness
in Students from Poverty* (Slocumb & Payne)

Bridges Out of Poverty: Strategies for Professionals and Communities
(Payne, DeVol, & Dreussi Smith)

What Every Church Member Should Know About Poverty (Ehlig & Payne)

Hidden Rules of Class at Work (Payne & Krabill)

Table of Contents

Dedication

Children's Bill of Rights

"The true measure of a nation's standing is how well it attends to its children—their health and safety, their material security, their education and socialization, and their sense of being loved, valued, and included in families and societies into which they are born."

—UNICEF, "Child Poverty in Perspective"

This is my Bill of Rights for Children.

Every Child Has the Right ...

- To be safe and reside in a violence-free environment

- To be nurtured and loved by at least one caring adult

- To have appropriate healthcare

- To have nutritious food every day

- To have stable shelter every night

- To have an education

Unqualified support for these rights is imperative to a healthy, safe society—indeed, to the future of our nation. Children are our future.

Introduction

The purpose of *Under-Resourced Learners: 8 Strategies to Boost Student Achievement* is to provide practical tools to educators to address the needs of under-resourced learners.

The first book I wrote, *A Framework for Understanding Poverty,* looked at resources as they related to the three economic classes: poverty, middle class, and wealth. Since that time, many individuals have said to me, "I know students who have so many things, but they aren't doing well in school." In this book I elaborate on that frame of reference and say that students can be resourced or under-resourced, regardless of money.

Under-Resourced Learners is intended to give some tangible tools to individuals who teach students in schools of the United States. UNICEF (an arm of the United Nations) uses resources as a measurement to determine stability, and it is legitimate. In the UNICEF report "An Overview of Child Well-Being in Rich Countries," the concept of resources is used to identify well-being. I would note that "under-resourced" is terminology directly from the United Nations and is a way to talk about students who don't have access to a number of the resources necessary for school success.

At the end of each chapter I present a series of practical steps you can take in relation to the strategies outlined in that chapter. You may wish to integrate them with techniques and strategies already working for you and your colleagues.

This book does not presume that schools can fix everything, so the focus necessarily is on the resources that can be developed in schools.

In the UNICEF report "Child Poverty in Perspective," the concept of resources is used to identify well-being. In the report, the European Union offers this definition of poverty: "The poor are those whose resources (material, cultural, and social) are so limited as to exclude them from the minimum acceptable way of life in the Member States in which they live" (page 6).

In this revised edition you will now find an *Under-Resourced Learners* study guide in Appendix A, and in Appendix D there are PowerPoint slides to use in teacher training. A number of the training strategies (charts, diagrams, and forms) are referenced earlier in the text of the book.

Strategy 1

Assess Resources of Individual Students to Determine Interventions

*"When I did my resources self-assessment, I realized that money was not my only problem. I always knew money wasn't going to solve all of my problems, but I thought it would solve most of the big ones. I realized that was not going to be true. It really hit me hard. I even had to step away from it for a few minutes because the reality of my situation hit me square in the face. It was one of those 'aha' moments— you know, the ones where you go 'Aha, **that's** why I've been doing that.' It was great and scary and heartbreaking and exhilarating and everything all at one moment. It was one of the hardest things I had to do but definitely the most beneficial. I now try to do a self-assessment about every six months to see what progress I've made."*

–Mary Gruza, Getting Ahead Graduate

"I've always believed that the Ruby Payne model explained why it was so important to examine the different resources that children and families have or don't have. The model also suggests various ways you can embed other resources to help children be more successful."

–Kelly Sharp, Sixth-Grade Language Arts/Social Studies Teacher

Why Look at Resources?

It isn't possible to educate well just by teaching the "group" and not knowing about the individual students in the classroom. Many students get identified as "at risk" when the issue is one of resources. When you know the resources of an individual, then you can determine the intervention(s) that will work best. Interventions that are successful work with the individual's strengths to enhance underdeveloped resources.

What Does It Mean to Be Under-Resourced? Is It a Personal Issue or a Situational Issue?

It is both. All individuals have an area or areas in their life where they would like to have more resources, i.e., more athletic abilities and better eyesight or be taller, shorter, smarter, quicker, etc.

For the purposes of this book, under-resourced is going to be defined as not having the resources to address a particular situation or negotiate a particular environment.

All resources are relative to the comparison group in which one finds oneself.

The good news is that resources can be developed—at any stage in life. *Under-Resourced Learners: 8 Strategies to Boost Student Achievement* is about how to do that.

For the purposes of this book, the following nine resources are going to be examined:

What Does It Look Like to Be Resourced? A Resourced Student Has Most or All of the Following Resources:

Financial

Having the money to purchase goods and services.

Language

Being able to speak and use formal register in writing and in speech.

Emotional

Being able to choose and control emotional responses, particularly to negative situations, without engaging in self-destructive behavior. This is an internal resource and shows itself through stamina, perseverance, and choices.

Mental

Having the mental abilities and acquired skills (reading, writing, computing) to deal with daily life.

Spiritual

Believing in divine purpose and guidance.

Physical

Having physical health and mobility.

Support Systems

Having friends, family, and backup resources available to access in times of need. These are external resources.

Relationships/Role Models

Having frequent access to adult(s) who are appropriate, who are nurturing to the child, and who do not engage in self-destructive behavior.

Knowledge of Hidden Rules

Knowing the unspoken cues and habits of a group.

Financial

▪ has the necessary school supplies	Yes	No
▪ has money for field trips	Yes	No
▪ has money for projects	Yes	No
▪ has food every evening and twice a day on weekends/holidays	Yes	No
▪ wears different clothing at least five days a week	Yes	No
▪ has more than one pair of shoes	Yes	No
▪ has a stable place to live (not a car, not a shelter, does not move every three months, is not moved from relative to relative)	Yes	No
▪ has own books	Yes	No
▪ has a place to study at home (includes good lighting and a table/desk)	Yes	No
▪ has had opportunities to participate in educational activities outside of school (e.g., museums, travel, camp)	Yes	No
▪ has access to transportation outside of school (e.g., subway, bus, household vehicle)	Yes	No

In the following true stories, what is the resource(s) available to the student? How could you intervene to develop additional resources and strengthen existing resources? Or is no intervention necessary?

- *A school had students in the fourth grade who were twins. One came to school one day and the other the next day. Everyone was convinced they were rotating days to take care of younger children. When it was finally investigated, the reality was that there was only one pair of shoes in the house. So they took turns wearing the shoes.*

- *A principal told me that when he was growing up, his family was so poor they only had one light bulb in the house. Each sibling got 15 minutes under the light to do homework every evening. If you didn't get your homework done in 15 minutes, then it didn't get finished at home because there was no light.*

- *One of the schools in the Houston area had to make a rule that parents could not come and feed the student's breakfast to themselves or a younger sibling. Parents were coming in to the school in the morning when students got free breakfast to feed themselves and another child.*

- *A young man I know in the United States has been to Europe four times, lived in Germany for three months, traveled to Australia and Tasmania, and has been to Mexico three times. He turned down a trip to China and Japan saying he had traveled enough. He had done all of this by the time he was 23 years old.*

Language

▪ can use the formal register of the language of the dominant culture	Yes	No
▪ can tell a story in chronological order	Yes	No
▪ can get to the point in a discussion	Yes	No
▪ can resolve a conflict using formal register	Yes	No
▪ can ask questions syntactically	Yes	No
▪ can write using formal organizational patterns for writing	Yes	No
▪ can use specific vocabulary in speech and writing	Yes	No
▪ can sort what is and is not important in nonfiction text	Yes	No
▪ can write a persuasive argument using support and logic	Yes	No

In the following true stories, what is the resource(s) available to the student? How could you intervene to develop additional resources and strengthen existing resources? Or is no intervention necessary?

- *A librarian was reading a story to a group of students about a young woman who was pretty, arrogant, and self-important. When she asked the students to tell her about the young woman, one of the boys said, "She thinks she's all that!" The librarian was upset with the student. Actually, he understood the character very well, but he could relay his understanding only in casual register.*

- *A student was in repeated trouble with the office for his behavior; the principal felt that the student was being evasive. Each time she would ask him for information, he would respond with one or two words: "It was nuthin'" or "I don't know." The principal was going to give strong consequences for the behavior, then learned it was simply about having very little vocabulary.*

- *One of the elementary schools in the Houston area has kindergarten students who have never seen a spoon and have no word for it.*

Emotional

• controls impulsivity most of the time	Yes	No
• can plan for behavior and assignments	Yes	No
• controls anger	Yes	No
• has positive self-talk	Yes	No
• sees the relationship between choice and consequence	Yes	No
• can resolve a problem with words (does not hit or become verbally abusive)	Yes	No
• can stay in formal register during an argument	Yes	No
• can predict outcomes based on cause and effect	Yes	No
• can separate the behavior (criticism) from the person (contempt)	Yes	No
• has the words to name feelings	Yes	No
• can use the adult voice	Yes	No

In the following true stories, what is the resource(s) available to the student? How could you intervene to develop additional resources and strengthen existing resources? Or is no intervention necessary?

- *I tutored three high school seniors who had failed the state exit exam several times and had only one more opportunity to pass it. When I gave them the skills test, they had the skills. They could read, understood the vocabulary, etc. Then I asked them if they had quit in the middle of the test, and all of them said yes. I asked them what they said to themselves and they replied:*

    "This test is stupid."

    "I'm cold."

    "I missed too many already."

    "I'm hungry."

    In other words, they had no positive self-talk, which is what people use to finish difficult tasks. I said to them, "Do you have a driver's license?" They all did. I told them, "When you get in that room and start the test, and you want to quit, say to yourself, 'If I can get a driver's license, then I can finish this test.'" Internal positive self-talk is a major tool and a key emotional resource.

- *When I was a principal, I had a student named Mary. She was in the office because she'd had a choke hold on another girl, Casandra, and was trying to bash her head into a brick wall. Mary explained that her mother had "paged her to her suite via intercom in their home on the golf course" the night before. Casandra had been angry with Mary the day before, so she had called Mary's mother and said that she (Casandra) was with Weight Watchers and that she (Mary's mother) had been recommended to them as a possible client because of her weight. Mary had been grounded by her mother because Mary's mother believed that Mary had instigated the call.*

Mental

• can read at a rate that doesn't interfere with meaning	Yes	No
• can read the material required for that grade level or task	Yes	No
• can write for the task as required by school or work	Yes	No
• can add, subtract, multiply, and divide	Yes	No
• can do the math as required by the grade level/course	Yes	No
• understands money as represented on paper—checkbooks, bank statements, etc.	Yes	No
• can operate in the paper world of school and work	Yes	No
• can use specific vocabulary related to the content or the job	Yes	No
• is test-savvy—knows how to take a test	Yes	No
• can develop questions over content or tasks on the job	Yes	No
• is organized and can find papers when they're needed (paper representation of space)	Yes	No
• can read a map	Yes	No
• has procedural self-talk	Yes	No
• can follow written directions	Yes	No
• can sequence a task or make a plan	Yes	No
• can represent an idea in a visual or a story (mental models)	Yes	No
• can prioritize tasks	Yes	No
• can sort what is and is not important in a task or a text (summarization)	Yes	No
• can divide tasks into parts	Yes	No
• can get tasks or projects done on time (paper representation of time)	Yes	No
• can make to-do lists or use a planner to get things done	Yes	No
• can use a calendar	Yes	No
• can tell how things are alike and different	Yes	No

In the following true stories, what is the resource(s) available to the student? How could you intervene to develop additional resources and strengthen existing resources? Or is no intervention necessary?

- *A parent was sent a form to be signed. The parent said she hadn't gotten the form. So the school sent it again by certified mail. The parent got angry and insisted that it had never come, even though she had signed for it. It turned out that the parent couldn't read.*

- *A 24-year-old man, college-educated, who had grown up in a home with few resources, was driving from Indiana to Ohio but suddenly turned north toward Michigan. When the passenger in the car asked him what he was doing, he said there was a road there, and he was using it. When the passenger explained that he was going north and not east, the young man said he had never used a map before because the household didn't have money for gas in order to travel. So there had never been a need for a map.*

Spiritual (Optimism and Hope)

has a future story for oneself personally	Yes	No
has hope for the future, i.e., believes that the future will work out in a positive way	Yes	No
believes in the personal ability to impact own life, i.e., does not believe future is fated	Yes	No
believes that there is extra support to help one with life, e.g., divine guidance, a set of beliefs, prayer, meditation, etc.	Yes	No
has a strong personal belief system about own positive value as a human being	Yes	No

In the following true stories, what is the resource(s) available to the student? How could you intervene to develop additional resources and strengthen existing resources? Or is no intervention necessary?

- *I was talking with an 18-year-old in alternative school and I asked him what his life would be like when he was 25. He said, "I will be dead." I asked him how he knew that, and he said everyone like him was dead.*

- *I knew a young lady who grew up in a very closed religious group. She counted down days from the time she was 13 years old until she was 18 years old and had graduated from high school. She knew that if she ran away she would never be able to have her future story.*

> - *A woman who became a teacher did so for this reason: Her fifth-grade teacher brought her family a turkey at Thanksgiving because he realized they didn't have food. She decided then that she would be a teacher because she would be able to help other students as this teacher did. Her teacher unknowingly gave her hope and a model for her future story.*

Physical

- has protein in diet on a daily basis (helps with memory and physical strength)	Yes	No
- is healthy (usually free of illness)	Yes	No
- gets sufficient sleep (6–8 hours of sleep per night)	Yes	No
- brushes teeth on a daily basis (high correlation between dental health and general health)	Yes	No
- has health insurance and/or access to preventive healthcare	Yes	No
- can see and hear well	Yes	No
- can move own body without help	Yes	No
- has high levels of energy and stamina	Yes	No
- can focus the energy on a task	Yes	No
- if a biochemical issue is present, it is addressed with either medication or a series of interventions	Yes	No
- does not use illegal drugs or alcohol	Yes	No
- engages in daily exercise	Yes	No
- has unstructured time each day to play/relax	Yes	No
- is physically fit	Yes	No
- is within the healthy weight/height range for age	Yes	No
- is free from physical and sexual abuse	Yes	No
- appearance is acceptable (clothes, hair, body are clean and presentable)	Yes	No

In the following true stories, what is the resource(s) available to the student? How could you intervene to develop additional resources and strengthen existing resources? Or is no intervention necessary?

> - *As principal, we had a first-grade girl who was in four activities every night (tennis, gymnastics, horse riding, cheerleading). The little girl was exhausted when she came to school in the morning. When we asked the mother if it would be possible to drop one activity, the mother said no—that her daughter needed these skills now.*

> - *One of the schools I worked in had a first-grade girl who came to school filthy every day. The social worker did a home visit and found there was a dirt floor and no running water. The school aide walked the girl over to the middle school every morning, let her take a shower in the girls' locker room, and had clean clothes for her to change into. At the end of the day, the girl put the clothes on she had come to school in. This same girl was asked for a math assignment to bring 100 of anything into school (100 beans, 100 stones, whatever). She brought in 100 scratched-off lottery tickets.*

Support Systems

- has parents who have at least five of the nine resources	Yes	No
- has parents who are supportive of school	Yes	No
- has at least caring and nurturing two adults	Yes	No
- has at least two friends (peers) who are nurturing and not destructive	Yes	No
- belongs to a peer group; can be racial, cultural, religious, activity-based, e.g., sports, music, academics	Yes	No
- is involved in one or more school activities (sports, music, theater, chess club, etc.)	Yes	No
- can make new friends (social capital)	Yes	No
- has at least two friends who are different from self (by race, culture, interest, academics, religion, etc.)	Yes	No
- is a mentor or a friend others come to for advice	Yes	No
- has at least two people who will be advocates	Yes	No
- is connected to a larger social network (bridging social capital— e.g., church, 4-H, Boys and Girls Club, soccer league, country club)	Yes	No
- can identify as a member of at least one group	Yes	No
- has at least one teacher or coach who knows the student personally and will be an advocate	Yes	No
- has at least one adult who is the support system for the household and not the child/student	Yes	No

In the following true stories, what is the resource(s) available to the student? How could you intervene to develop additional resources and strengthen existing resources? Or is no intervention necessary?

- *A college professor told me that she grew up in a household where she was the support system for the household. Her father left the family, and she was the oldest child. Her mother worked two jobs. She became the mother and the caretaker of four younger siblings. She said it created a difficult relationship between her and her mother and robbed her of her childhood. When the child is the support system for the household, the time to develop a support system for oneself, the time to learn, the time to have friends are severely limited.*

- *A high school teacher told me that his father was a drug addict and physically abusive. His father beat him badly in January, left him in the freezing rain injured and bleeding, and told his mother that if she helped her son, he (the father) would blow her brains out. He left home at 15 and lived on his own. He joined the military. When he retired from the military, he became a teacher. He married at 17 and said his wife became his main support system.*

- *A young Vietnamese immigrant told me that he left home at age 10 alone in a small boat with some other people. He lived in a refugee camp for years.*

Relationships/Role Models

- has at least two friends own age	Yes	No
- has at least one adult on the staff who knows the student	Yes	No
- has at least two adults outside of school who care about the student	Yes	No
- admires at least one person	Yes	No
- admires at least one person who is not a sports figure or an entertainment celebrity	Yes	No
- can identify the admirable traits in a role model	Yes	No
- can identify negative role models	Yes	No
- knows how to make friendships and relationships that are positive and not destructive	Yes	No
- can give and accept a compliment	Yes	No

(continued on next page)

Relationships/Role Models (continued from previous page)

▪ has access to individuals who have positive and non-destructive success in the dominant culture but also have retained their cultural/ racial roots	Yes	No
▪ knows the history and examples of successful individuals in own family or racial/cultural past	Yes	No
▪ has role identity	Yes	No
▪ has an individual who can be trusted	Yes	No

In the following true stories, what is the resource(s) available to the student? How could you intervene to develop additional resources and strengthen existing resources? Or is no intervention necessary?

- *A young minority man changed his life at 19 because he met a lawyer who looked like him and was a member of his race. The lawyer was very successful, and the young man was invited to the lawyer's home. He loved the home and decided he would have one just like it. He went on to college and is now quite successful.*

- *A highly successful CEO, Al, who grew up very poor, told me that he had a high school coach who became his college coach in basketball. His junior year of college, Al went out one night and played basketball with a local league when he should have been studying. That night when he got back to his dorm, there was a sign on his door that said, "Come see me." He went to the coach's office, but it was midnight, and the coach wasn't there. The next morning at 6 a.m. Al was waiting for the coach at his office. When the coach came, he asked Al where he had been the night before. Al told him. Then the coach asked who was there. He told him. The coach said, "All of those men have incredible talent. All of those men are pumping gas or flipping burgers because they did what you did. They played ball instead of studying. If you don't want to pump gas or flip burgers, it's not enough to have talent, you also must be educated." At first Al was furious. But as he thought about what the coach said, he realized it was true. And so, along with his basketball, he also studied.*

Knowledge of Hidden Rules

▪ can identify and avoid the "pet peeves" of the person in charge, i.e., boss, teacher, et al.	Yes	No
▪ can identify at school or work what will actually get you into trouble versus what the rules say will get you into trouble	Yes	No
▪ is successful with different teachers, students, bosses	Yes	No
▪ can work/learn from someone who is not liked	Yes	No
▪ can assess a situation for what behaviors can be used and which ones cannot for success in that situation or with that person	Yes	No
▪ can articulate what the hidden rules are in a given situation or with a given person	Yes	No
▪ can differentiate between the "real" authority and the stated authority in a given situation	Yes	No
▪ knows the hidden rules of the school environment	Yes	No
▪ knows the hidden rules of the work environment	Yes	No
▪ can assess the unspoken cueing mechanisms in a given situation or with a given person and use that information advantageously	Yes	No

In the following true stories, what is the resource(s) available to the student? How could you intervene to develop additional resources and strengthen existing resources? Or is no intervention necessary?

- *A young man in college realized that one of his professors looked at only the students in the first three rows of the auditorium. The professor's eyes never went beyond that third row. So the student moved into one of the first three rows so that the professor would see him and know that he was there.*

- *A middle school teacher told me he teaches his students "how to get the teacher to do whatever they want." He then teaches them the hidden rules of cooperation and working with the teacher—instead of against them—in order to get what they want. In other words, he teaches them the hidden rules of working with authority.*

Do We Assess the Resources of the Individual or the Household?

When working with children, we look at the resources of the household. When working with adolescents and adults, we look at the individual and the larger support system to which the individual has access.

Why look at resources?

Because they tell us where to make interventions.

Where do we start with interventions?

We work from strengths.

Why look at relationships first?

Because they are a primary motivation for learning.

How do we know what the resources are?

One of the big questions is how do we find out the resources that an individual has without being intrusive. There are several ways to do this.

Techniques for Elementary Students

1. **Draw a picture.**

   After drawing a picture of their household, students orally tell you a story about the picture. What is not in the picture is as important as what is in the picture.

2. **Tell stories.**

   Elementary students often like to tell stories.

3. **Do journal writing.**

   Have them do a journal entry—e.g., My favorite adult is _____ and why. My favorite teacher is _____ and why. My favorite book is _____ and why. You might add favorite food, TV show, video game, story, etc.

Techniques for Secondary Students

1. Share experiences.

At the beginning of the year, tell students about yourself, your credentials, and what you hope they learn during the year. Then ask them to write back to you and tell you things that would help you teach them. Do they work after school? What do they like about school? What do they hate? What helps them learn? Etc.

2. Have individual conferences.

One high school teacher gave an independent assignment every Friday. He called students up to his desk one at a time, went over their grades with them, asked if there was anything he could do to help them with the class. Behavior improved tremendously; grades also went up.

3. Write about oneself.

Use this fill-in-the-blanks exercise to help students with self-disclosure.

Title

I have always liked/disliked my name, _____

because _____. I was born on _____

and am currently _____ years old. Some people may think my life is _____

_____, but I feel that I have _____ to share with others.

I have a _____ family. Counting me, there are _____

people living in my house. The adults' names are _____

_____, and the children's names are _____

_____.

At home, I would consider _____

my confidant(s) because I can trust them and know that no matter what, they will

always be there for me.

I have several interests and hobbies (for example, I keep myself busy _____

_____).

(continued on next page)

(continued from previous page)

I also like to watch sports like _____, but I really like playing _____. These are my favorites because _____. After school and on weekends, I work at _____ from _____ to _____. This is a good/not so good job because _____.

I participate in extracurricular activities/clubs at school; my favorite one is _____ _____, and I have been a member for _____. I attend/do not attend church at _____. All of these activities have helped me become a better person in my community.

School makes me feel _____. My best subject is _____, and my least-favorite subject would have to be _____ because _____. In math I usually make _____ grades, and in language arts I make _____ grades. I like/do not like to read, but/and my favorite book I ever read is titled _____. Additionally, I am/am not a good writer. If I have a choice between writing fiction or non-fiction, I choose _____ because _____ _____. School is the _____ of the day for me.

My personality is best described by the word _____. It's obvious that I am/am not a hard worker because _____ _____. When I get angry, I _____ _____, but you'll know when I'm happy because _____ _____. Most of the time, I make _____ decisions because I base them on _____. If I were to get angry at school and needed to "cool down," I would go to _____ _____ because _____.

When I have good news to share, _____ is the first

(continued on next page)

(continued from previous page)

person I call. I know I can always get help with my homework or help to study for a test from _____. These people have helped me in the past and will continue to help me grow.

I would describe a role model as a person who _____ _____. The person or people I respect the most are _____ because they treat me _____ _____ (for example, _____ _____). I think they might be honored to know that I admire them as much as I do; one way I could let them know is by _____.

My plans for the future will depend on _____ _____. My objective after high school is to _____ _____.

When I graduate, I want to _____ _____ because _____ _____. I would like to leave behind the legacy of _____ _____(for example, _____ _____).

I know that I can eventually contribute to my community and society if I work hard now; the uphill struggles and difficulties I encounter along the way will pay off in the end.

Adapted from materials developed by JuDee Hancock, educational consultant.

Do You Assess the Resources of Every Student?

No. You assess the resources of the students who are having difficulty with achievement or success in school.

Steps to Follow

1. Identify students for whom concerns exist or achievement is lagging.

2. Assess the resources of the student based on the information that you have. You may solicit the assistance of a counselor, assistant principal, social worker, et al., to determine the resource base. Some schools use a team approach.

3. Determine the strengths of the student, i.e., what resources are available? Also determine what resources are not available or could be developed.

4. Start with the strongest resource and identify an intervention that will work. For example, if the student has a strong parental resource base, then that is a support system that can help the student. But if a student doesn't have a strong support system, then telling the parent to help with homework will not occur. If this same student has a strong emotional resource base, then the student could be given tools to be able to get the homework done.

Strategy ❷

Build Relationships of Mutual Respect with Students

Utilize relational learning in the classroom

"Building relationships with the students is probably the most important piece for me of the whole Ruby Payne Model. The students who are typically at our school may not have any other positive relationships in their lives, and they may not trust anyone else. That's not necessarily true of everyone, but many times students who are low-performing have not trusted a teacher and therefore they wouldn't perform. Maybe they had it up there all along, but they didn't want to give that part up.

"The relationship-building piece of what Ruby Payne has taught me is critical. I think that's the bottom line. I don't think you can move on without it. I think you have to do that, first and foremost, and if that takes a year to do, then that's sometimes what you have to work on with some of these kids. For a year maybe you just build those relationships, and then you can move on.

"We had this one girl who was tough as nails. When she came to us, she was rotten. She was just tough; she fought on the street all the time, because at home she was the parent of her household. And she fought her way through seventh grade (our team had her in seventh and eighth grades), but our team kept building relationships unconditionally. We (our team) unconditionally loved her. We said, 'You can't do this, we are going to punish you, write you up on a long form, you're punished, and here are the consequences.' But we didn't give up on her, and we continued to do that. She came back to us in eighth grade, and she still had that attitude, but it was changing, slowly but surely.

"And, oh, in October of that second year she told me a story. Now I am not typically very sensitive, I mean, I am, but I don't cry easily. So she started telling me the story, and my team teacher and I were talking to her, and the student started crying, and it was really sad, and it made me cry. So I grabbed a tissue, dabbed my eyes, we hugged, and it was all good. We got a letter back from her, a little note (the little contraband notes we get from time to time). And she's in high school doing well, and the last line of it—it almost makes me cry again—and it said, 'Miss Murdaugh, do you remember when I told you the story, and it made you cry? I have the tissue hanging in my locker in high school.' So that's what we do. That's not what I do, that's what we do; that's what Ruby's taught us to do. So it's working.

"It was very different from what I had been doing, from the way I had taught in the past. I think in the past I had good days and bad days, and it was very hit or miss really. Sometimes I had very good years and connected with some students, and sometimes I didn't. But it wasn't consistent, and I could never really figure out what I was doing right or what I was doing wrong. The Ruby Payne models have really made it concrete to me. It's clear. I've taught 27 years now, and I don't want to stop yet; I'm just getting good. My girls are grown now. They're saying, 'OK, Mom, come on home,' but, oh no ... I wish I would've learned all this years ago. It's making a big difference. I think I'm doing more now for students than I've ever done."

–Dottie Murdaugh, Middle School Teacher

What Is Relational Learning?

Relational learning has seven characteristics:

1. Relationships of mutual respect with teachers and administrators

2. A peer group to belong to that is positive and not destructive

3. A coach or advocate who helps the student

4. If not a member of the dominant culture, the student has access to individuals (or histories of individuals) who have attained success and retained connections to their roots

5. Bridging social capital * (social-media contacts, mentors, et al.) to the larger society

6. At the secondary level, a very specific and clear plan for addressing own learning performance

7. A safe environment (emotionally, verbally, and physically)

* Social capital is terminology used by Robert Putnam in his book *Bowling Alone*. It basically means who you know. He identifies two kinds—bonding and bridging. **Bonding** social capital involves people who are like you; **bridging** social capital involves people different from you.

More detail on each of the seven points above is provided later in this chapter, beginning on page 30.

In *Social Intelligence* Daniel Goleman states:

> *In a study of 910 first graders from a national sample representative of the entire United States, trained observers evaluated their teachers, and assessed the effect of teaching style on how well the at-risk children learned. The best results were found when teachers: (a) tuned into the child and responded to his needs, moods, interests, and capabilities, letting them guide their interactions, (b) created an upbeat classroom climate with pleasant conversations, lots of laughter and excitement, (c) showed warmth and "positive regard" for students, (d) had classroom management, with clear but flexible expectations and routines, so that students followed rules largely on their own.*

> *Students who were already doing well continued to do so regardless of the setting. But at-risk students who had cold or controlling teachers floundered academically—even when their teachers followed pedagogic guidelines for good instruction. Yet the study found a stunning difference among the at-risk students: if they had a warm, responsive teacher, they flourished, learning as well as the other kids ...*
>
> *By offering a secure base, a teacher creates an environment that lets students' brains function at their best. That base becomes a safe haven, a zone of strength from which they can venture forth to explore, to master something new, to achieve (pages 282–283).*

Why Are Relationships So *Essential* to Learning?

All learning is double-coded—cognitively *and* emotionally (more on that on page 25 where the work of Stanley Greenspan and Beryl Benderly is addressed). Relationships constitute the primary motivation for almost all learning.

These relationships occur within a context of mutual respect, which involves three things: high expectations, insistence, and support. It isn't about being a "friend" or "buddy" but about mutual respect.

You may have heard this statement: *"Children don't care how much you know until they know how much you care."* Indeed, caring is the foundation of relationships.

Here is what students tell us they look for to determine mutual respect:

Issue	Evidenced	Needed	Not applicable
Teacher calls students by name.			
Teacher uses courtesies: "please," "thank you," etc.			
Students use courtesies with each other and with teacher.			
Teacher calls on all students.			
Teacher gets into proximity (within an arm's reach) of all students—daily if possible, but at least weekly.			
Teacher greets students at door.			
Teacher smiles at students.			
Classroom has businesslike atmosphere.			

(continued on next page)

(continued from previous page)

Issue	Evidenced	Needed	Not applicable
Students are given tools to assess/evaluate own work.			
Student-generated questions are used as part of instruction.			
Grading/scoring is clear and easily understood.			
Students may ask for extra help from teacher.			

In the research it's called "school connectedness" as noted in the material below.

Students are more likely to succeed when they feel connected to school. School connection is the belief by students that adults in the school care about their learning, as well as about them as individuals. The key requirements for feeling connected include students' experiencing:

- High academic expectations and rigor coupled with support for learning
- Positive adult-student relationships
- Safety: both physical and emotional

Increasing the number of students connected to school is likely to impact critical accountability measures, such as:

- Academic performance
- Incidents of fighting, bullying, or vandalism
- Absenteeism
- School completion rates

Strong scientific evidence demonstrates that increased student connection to school promotes:

- Educational motivation
- Classroom attendance
- Improved school attendance

Source: University of Minnesota. Division of General Pediatrics and Adolescent Health.

Mutual respect is taught, it is earned, it is reciprocated, and it is insisted upon by the teacher. However, students will not automatically respect a teacher just because the teacher insists upon respect.

It also must be earned.

"I received this on a note the other day, and I quote, 'You are mean and want us to fail. How are you still my favorite teacher?' I thought that was just priceless. I'm going to take that home and keep it forever."

–Darl Collins, High School Chemistry Teacher

Motivation for Learning

Probably the most frequently asked question by teachers is this: How can I get my students to want to learn? Dr. James Comer of Yale University says it best:

No significant learning occurs without a significant relationship [of mutual respect].

Learning requires human interaction. At the heart of all learning are relationships.

How do you recognize relationships of mutual respect?

Generally, in relationships of mutual respect, three things are present:

Support, insistence, and high expectations

In *The Growth of the Mind and the Endangered Origins of Intelligence*, Greenspan and Benderly say all learning is double-coded, both mentally and emotionally. How you feel about something is part of the learning and your openness to the learning.

It is very important to understand the emotional underpinnings of learning. Most learning is in essence emotional (our most vivid memories have an emotional component), and virtually all learning starts with significant relationships.

Six Developmental Stages in the Learning Process

Six developmental stages in the learning process occur when relationships are supportive and nurturing. And the primary motivator for the development of each stage is a significant relationship. These six stages are:

Stage	Explanation
1. Ability to attend	To pay attention to the sensory data in the environment. The earliest sensory data—touch, taste, sound, smell, sight—result from the interplay of relationships.
2. Ability to engage	To experience feelings—joy, pleasure, anger, emotional warmth, disappointment, assertiveness, etc. Intimacy and relating begin at this stage.
3. Ability to be intentional	To create and direct desire. To use non-verbals with purpose and intention. For example, I (as an infant) want you to hold me, so I hold up my arms, and you pick me up.
4. Ability to form complex interactive patterns	To connect and use one's own intentional signals in interaction with another to negotiate and to receive security, acceptance, and approval.
5. Ability to create images, symbols, and ideas	To give abstract mental constructs emotional meaning and significance. This is the basis of reasoning and emotion-based coping strategies. When images, symbols, and ideas don't have emotional investment, they are fragmented.
6. Ability to connect images, symbols, and ideas	To develop the infrastructure and architecture of the mind. To "image" one's own feelings and desires and to understand emotional signals from others.

In discussing the six stages, one overriding reality must be remembered:

Emotion organizes experience and behavior.

STAGE 1: Ability to Attend

At the very beginning of learning, the infant must sort out what the sensations are and what they mean. Those earliest sensations almost always come through relationships. Someone is holding the child. Someone is feeding the child. The child must stay calm enough to notice the sensations the child is experiencing. The child must find patterns in the sensations. From these patterns come security and order. From this security and order comes the ability to regulate the mind.

STAGE 2: Ability to Engage

When young children can attend to the surroundings and actions of the people who are their caretakers, they become engaged. The caretaker smiles, and they smile. In short, the child mirrors the expressions of the caretaker.

Greenspan and Benderly say it well:

> *Without some degree of this ecstatic wooing by at least one adult who adores her, a child may never know the powerful intoxication of human closeness, never abandon herself to the magnetic pull of human relationships ... Whether because her nervous system is unable to sustain the sensations of early love or her caregiver is unable to convey them, such a child is at risk of becoming self-absorbed or an unfeeling, self-centered, aggressive individual who can inflict injury without qualm or remorse (page 51).*

STAGE 3: Ability to Be Intentional

At this preverbal stage, a purposeful exchange of signals and responses is used to elicit what the child desires. In this stage the child learns to distinguish between you and me, i.e., from self and other. Boundaries are established. When responses are inappropriate, the child becomes disorganized and eventually loses interest. For example, if a person is talking to someone with a "poker face," eventually the conversation becomes fragmented; the speaker loses interest and gives up.

Interactions become purposeful, and "willful reciprocity" occurs, which also signals a higher developmental level of the central nervous system.

Desires or wishes are tied to actions, not ideas. Desires or wishes also are linked to subjective needs, not objective needs.

STAGE 4: Ability to Form Complex Interactive Patterns

At this stage, purpose and interaction become the focus. The child learns to communicate across space, i.e., I am not touching my caregiver. She is in the next room, but I know she is there. This gives a strong sense of emotional security. Imitation is a part of this stage. The child mimics what the adult does. At this stage, a child's emotions are attached to patterns of response. Attitudes and values start here. Meaning is established from patterns of desire, expectation, and intention.

STAGE 5: Ability to Create Images, Symbols, and Ideas

Here children experience themselves in images—and not just in feelings, physical sensations, and behavior. It's important to note that youngsters who haven't mastered the previous stages tend to operate in a concrete, rote manner. At this point in time, individuals can try out behaviors and actions inside their head without actually doing them.

STAGE 6: Ability to Connect Images, Symbols, and Ideas

At this stage, the individual connects the images, symbols, and ideas that were developed in Stage 5 to an architecture in which abstractions are emotionally embedded and interwoven. The individual is able to view emotions abstractly and work through them both at a thinking level and a feeling one. In other words, sorting occurs both cognitively and through emotion.

How does this knowledge of stages affect your understanding of students in your classroom? Does it help explain some of the student behaviors?

Because schools and the work setting operate at Stages 5 and 6, many individuals are new learners to the abstract.

How do students know that teachers have respect for them?

Two pieces of research are particularly instructive. One is from Stephen Covey, and the other is research by TESA (Teacher Expectations and Student Achievement).

Covey states that relationships of mutual respect are like bank accounts. You make emotional deposits to those relationships, and you make emotional withdrawals from the relationships. When the withdrawals are substantially greater than the deposits, the relationship is soon broken.

Deposits	Withdrawals
Seek first to understand	Seek first to be understood
Keeping promises	Breaking promises
Kindnesses, courtesies	Unkindnesses, discourtesies
Clarifying expectations	Violating expectations
Loyalty to the absent	Disloyalty, duplicity
Apologies	Pride, conceit, arrogance
Open to feedback	Rejecting feedback

Source: Adapted from *The Seven Habits of Highly Effective People* by Stephen Covey.

The TESA research describes 15 behaviors that teachers use with students when there is mutual respect between teacher and student. The study found that when these behaviors are used with all students, learning jumps dramatically.

Here are the 15 behaviors of mutual respect:

1. Calls on everyone in the room equitably.
2. Provides individual help.
3. Gives "wait time" (allows student enough time to answer).
4. Asks questions to give the student clues about the answer.
5. Asks questions that require more thought.
6. Tells students whether their answers are right or wrong.
7. Gives specific praise.
8. Gives reasons for praise.
9. Listens.
10. Accepts the feelings of the student.

11. Gets within an arm's reach of each student each day.

12. Is courteous to students.

13. Shows personal interest and gives compliments.

14. Touches students (appropriately).

15. Desists (does not call attention to every misbehavior).

Source: TESA (Teacher Education and Student Achievement). Los Angeles Board of Education.

When we asked students in our research how they knew the teacher had respect for them, repeatedly we heard the following:

- The teacher calls me by my name, not "Hey you."

- The teacher answers my questions.

- The teacher cares about me.

- The teacher talks to me with respect.

- The teacher notices me and says hi.

- The teacher helps me when I need help.

What Does This Mean in Practice?

If a student and teacher don't have a relationship of mutual respect, the learning will be significantly reduced and, for some students, it won't occur at all.

If a student and teacher don't like each other—or even come to despise each other—forget about significant, positive learning. If mutual respect is present, that can compensate for the dislike.

How Do Teachers Build Mutual Respect?

"Relationships of mutual respect are built not in one day but over a period of time. I approach it like caring and sharing, like being honest and firm: holding the student accountable. When students realize how important all these things are, then the relationship begins to build."

–Darl Collins, High School Chemistry Teacher

Mutual respect is as much about non-verbals as it is about what you say.

A question I frequently get is: "Can you please give me a list of things to do?"

It's not necessarily about things to do. It's as much about non-verbals as it is anything else. Non-verbals are based upon intent. If you go into a conversation with the intent to win, that will be reflected in your non-verbals. If you go into a conversation with the intent to understand, that will be reflected as well. Voice tone is a huge issue in conversations and comments. You can say "Help me understand" with sarcasm or with caring. Even though the words are the same, the meaning is very different.

The second issue is that when you care about people, you hold them accountable. You don't let them do things that will hurt them or you—if at all possible. (Sometimes it isn't possible to stop self-destructive behavior.) It may be as simple as saying, "You may not do that here" and then enforcing that. What good teachers, administrators, and parents know is that it's far more difficult to hold young people accountable than it is to let them simply do as they please. So it's also about being firm, caring, and consistent.

What Are the Strategies for Building Relational Learning?

1. **Relationships of mutual respect with teachers and administrators**

    Several examples have already been given on pages 28 and 29: Covey's seven points, TESA's 15 behaviors, and the six things cited by students.

2. **A peer group to belong to that is positive and not destructive**

    There are students who go through a complete day of school and don't speak with anyone. Several of the school shootings and many behavior problems at school have to do with students who are "isolates." This isolation from others leads to a sense of not belonging. Belonging is a basic human need, as Abraham Maslow identified years ago in his "hierarchy of needs."

How do you help students belong?

a. Try to make sure that no child plays alone at recess. Assign another child to be that student's buddy for one day.

b. Have students work in pairs at least once a day. They each hand in their own work, but they must interact with each other (collaborative learning) in order to get the assignment done.

c. Each student is assigned to a group that meets once a week during lunch or after school. It should be based on the student's interests. It is particularly vital in middle school and in the ninth-grade year of high school. It can be a chess club, flag corps, rocketry club, another after-school club, intramural sports, etc.

d. Part of extra tutoring or instruction occurs in small groups of two or three. The students work to teach each other, as well as being instructed.

3. A coach or advocate who helps the student

One of the characteristics of many successful students is that they have an advocate—someone who gives them a voice and who is there to advocate for them. Many students have their advocates or coaches in the form of parents or someone in their external support system. But students whose support systems or relationships are under-resourced need a coach or advocate through school. What are some ways schools do that?

a. Ask interested teachers (don't assign this because it usually backfires) if they would take one student and meet with that student every day for five minutes. They ask how the student is doing. Does the student need help? Is the student having trouble? What's going on in the student's life?

b. Have student advocates at the secondary level—middle and high school. These student advocates meet with the students most in danger of failing and develop a plan to meet each student's goals. If there's a major personality conflict between a student and a particular teacher, sometimes the advocate can help identify this— and the student can then be allowed to transfer to another class and teacher.

4. **If not a member of the dominant culture, the student has access to individuals (or histories of individuals) who have attained success and retained connections to their roots**

Most curriculum concentrates on the accomplishments of the dominant culture. Students who are not members of the dominant culture often know very little about the history or accomplishments of their own heritage.

An educator friend of mine, who is minority, told me that she couldn't get her son interested in reading. One day he saw a book that had people in it who looked like him, and he was thrilled. He told his mother that the book was about him. Then he wanted to learn to read.

a. If this information is not in the textbooks, then it becomes part of the course through student research and projects, teacher infusion, etc. Teachers often tell me they don't have time to do the research. In that case, students can research the missing information as part of project.

b. Encourage students to take pictures in their own households of individuals who do things that are helpful. Have students create a scrapbook of these pictures and caption them with what is happening.

c. Have the class generate a list of what "success" is. Is it money, public acclaim, caring for individuals less fortunate, a fabulous teacher, a sports figure, a movie star??

d. For secondary students, particularly in social studies or history, a fascinating discussion is whether it's possible to attain success and still stay connected to your roots. If so, how? Do they know anyone who has done it?

e. Have guest speakers who aren't from the dominant culture address an aspect of literature, history, music, or art.

f. Have students write a future story as a movie script about what they will do as adults, what they will look like, how they will make a difference and be known.

g. Make sure your school library reflects the cultural background and languages of the students in your classroom.

5. **Bridging social capital (e-mail, texting, social media contacts, mentors, et al.) to the larger society**

   Bridging social capital is Robert Putnam's terminology, meaning people you know who are different from you. It is from people different from you that much learning occurs. *Bonding social capital* involves people you know who are like you.

   a. One way to do it is with e-mail; texting; and selected, approved social-media contacts. They can be from another country, another part of this country, adults from the business community, or individuals from the non-profit community. The person is to provide information and support out of a much larger context. The e-mails always need to be copied to a school person. If the e-mail buddy is local, a meeting needs to take place with the buddy, the student and the school person. If the e-mail buddy is from another country or another part of the state or nation, the relationship will get set up only on recommendation of a school person.

   b. Mentors are another way. One issue with mentors is that it's difficult to find mentors, particularly when they're supposed to come only at a certain time on a certain day. It usually needs to be more flexible to work with the mentor's schedule. It's better to ask if they can meet with the person once a week for at least 30 minutes. Again, these meetings must be supervised or in a public place.

   c. Mentoring *by* the student is another way and is very powerful. The older student becomes a mentor to a younger student.

6. **At the secondary level, a very specific and clear plan for addressing the student's own learning performance**

   The more clearly the expected end result is identified, the better the outcome and performance. Often guidance counselors do this at the secondary level, but it tends to be fairly perfunctory, given the demands on their time.

   a. To help students pass the state assessment, a teacher did the following and was very successful. All her students took a mock test in math. Then they scored their own papers. They made this grid:

Questions I got right and could get right again	Questions I did or did not do correctly but am not sure how to do	Questions where I had no clue

In the top row, for each category, students wrote the numbers of the test questions and the objective it went with. Then they identified strategies that could be used with each objective. As they went through the questions, in the second row of boxes, they identified where they would put it, e.g., "no clue" got moved to "I know I could get it right." We identified for students how many they had to get right to pass. The students then went back and counted how many questions were in each category and recalculated what they thought their performance would be. Then they took another sample or mock test and refigured how they actually did. This is self-advocacy and provides tools for addressing a task.

b. Another example is to provide rubrics for self-assessment.

Rubric to Measure a Skilled Musician (in Band and Orchestra)

Criteria	1	2	3	4
Accuracy	Not in time Several wrong notes Wrong key	Mostly in correct time Misses notes Key is correct Fingerings are off	In correct time Mostly uses correct fingerings Notes are correct	Timing is virtually always correct Fingerings are correct Notes are virtually always correct
Articulation	No variation in tempo Markings not observed No contrast in sound	Some variation in tempo but not correct Some contrast but incorrect for piece Random use of markings	Tempo mostly correct Mostly correct use of markings Dynamic contrast thin but correct	Markings are virtually always observed and followed Wide range of dynamic contrast Tempo is correct

(continued on next page)

(continued from previous page)

Criteria	1	2	3	4
Sound quality	Thin timbre High and low notes are off Too loud or too soft for note or section Unpleasant to ear	Timbre for most notes is fuller All difficult notes have some timbre Use of sound markings is random	Timbre is mostly full Sound markings are used but not advantageously	Timbre is full Sound markings are correctly interpreted and followed
Interpretation	No meaning assigned to piece No understanding of intent or purpose of composer	Playing indicates emotion but little understanding of meaning Understands that piece has climax but does not know where it is	Playing mostly conveys meaning and always conveys emotion Understands role of climax Can talk about intent and purpose	Playing conveys meaning and emotion Climax can be identified Plays truly to intent and purpose
Ensemble contribution	Does not pay attention to conductor Listens only to own playing Too loud/soft for group	Periodically pays attention to conductor Is mostly in balance with group Listens to own section Has little understanding of own contribution to melody	Mostly follows conductor's interpretations In balance with group Mostly listens to piece as whole Can verbally articulate contribution to melody but does not always reflect that in playing	Follows conductor's interpretation In balance with group Listens to piece as whole Understands own contribution to melody

An Orchestra teacher and I developed this to help his students better identify what a skilled musician would be. After a performance, the students highlighted in one color what they thought their performance was. The teacher highlighted in another color what he thought their performance was, after which the students made plans to address the discrepancy.

7. A safe environment (emotionally, verbally, and physically)

Learning levels are much higher when there is safety. Sarcasm and verbal abuse (particularly when it involves authority, and only one person in the interaction is allowed to engage in it) creates latent hostility. The research on latent hostility is that it permeates organizations and impacts individuals for *decades*.

a. Identify tactics of verbal disrespect. What follows is a chart of tactics and examples.

Verbal Disrespect

Type	Definition	Examples of exchanges between teachers or administrators and students
Withholding	To remain cool and indifferent, to be silent and aloof, to reveal as little as possible.	"What do you want me to say?" "Why should I care if you like it?" "I don't have to tell you how to do it." "I don't have to answer your question."
Countering	To express the opposite of what the person says.	"This assignment is hard." "No, it's not. It's easy." "You're not fair." "Yes, I am."
Disguising as a joke	To make disparaging comments disguised as a joke.	"You couldn't find your head if it wasn't attached." "You're so ugly even a mother couldn't love you." "When God was giving out brains, you thought he said trains, and you got in the wrong line!"
Blocking and diverting	To prevent the conversation from continuing, often by switching the topic.	"You're just trying to have the last word." "You heard me. I shouldn't have to repeat myself." "That's a lot of crap!" "Did anybody ask you?" "Will you get off my back?"
Accusing and blaming	To blame the other person for one's own anger, irritation, or insecurity.	"You're looking for trouble." "You're just trying to pick a fight." "You don't care about me."

(continued on next page)

(continued from previous page)

Type	Definition	Examples of exchanges between teachers or administrators and students
Judging and criticizing	To judge and express the judgment in a negative, critical way. To judge a third person and express it in a negative, critical way.	"You're stupid." "You're lazy." "You're an awful teacher." "She can't keep anything straight."
Trivializing	To diminish and make insignificant the work or contribution of the other person.	"I know you helped me do the problem, but you should have given me the answer." "I realize you did the work yourself, but did you have to write your name that big?"
Undermining	To dampen interest and enthusiasm by eroding confidence.	"Really, I don't know anyone who would be interested in that." "What makes you think you're so smart?" "Couldn't you find a more boring topic?" "Who are you trying to impress?" "Did you really go to college?"
Threatening	To manipulate by threatening loss or pain.	"Do that again, and I'll kick you out." "My mom's going to call you." "You'll flunk this class." "You mess with me, and my dad will get you."
Name calling	To call the other person by names, including terms of endearment that are said sarcastically.	"Well, darling …" "You're a bitch!" "You're a troublemaker!"
Forgetting	To forget incidents, promises, and agreements for the purpose of manipulation.	"I don't know what you're talking about." "I never agreed to that!" "I never promised to behave."
Ordering	To give orders instead of asking respectfully.	"Do your work and shut up." "Quit looking at me."
Denying	To deny the reality of the other person.	"You made that up." "You're crazy." "Where did you get that?" "I never said that. I never did that."

(continued on next page)

(continued from previous page)

Type	Definition	Examples of exchanges between teachers or administrators and students
Abusive anger	To use anger, both verbally and non-verbally, in unpredictable outbursts to put the blame for own inadequacies on the other person. It includes verbal rage, snapping at person, and shouting. It is part of the anger addiction cycle in which the person releases inner tension. It can be triggered by changes at home or school, fears, the current sense of power, feelings of dependency or inadequacy, or unmet needs.	Teacher: "Why didn't the homework get done?" Student: "You're a bitch!" (Gets up and stomps out of the room.) Student: "I don't understand." Teacher (throws down pencil and yells): "You never understand! Why are you in this class anyway?"

Source: Adapted from *The Verbally Abusive Relationship: How to Recognize It and How to Respond* by Patricia Evans.

b. One high school had students signing a contract agreeing to help make the school safe. It included aspects of their own behavior (i.e., not bringing weapons, not bullying, etc.) but also aspects of alerting school officials to dangerous behavior.

c. Helping students become better friends. One school did the following: Students were asked to identify their best friends, along with the issues they discussed with best friends. Then they tallied the names of best friends and took the top tallied names and gave them a day of training on how to be better friends—how to not give advice, how to ask questions, how to report really serious issues to an adult (clinical depression, suicide threats, etc.).

d. Peer mediation is another tool.

e. At the secondary level, keep students moving during lunch. More than one secondary school doesn't let students stand in groups during lunch because that's where fights tend to start. They have a "walking and talking" rule.

In *The Art and Science of Teaching*, Robert Marzano identifies the following action steps that communicate an appropriate level of concern and cooperation (pages 154–161):

a. Know something about each student.

b. Engage in behaviors that indicate affection for each student.

c. Bring student interests into content and personalize learning activities.

d. Engage in physical behaviors that communicate interest in students.

e. Use humor when appropriate.

f. Consistently enforce positive and negative consequences.

Steps to Follow

1. Make sure every student has at least one adult in the building who touches base with the student once a day and cares about the student.

2. Ensure that all students have a peer or peer group with whom they can talk during an academic task every day.

3. Make sure that no child plays alone at recess for more than one day and that no secondary student eats lunch alone.

4. Assign every student to some type of extracurricular activity so that there is a sense of belonging.

5. Ensure that, within the academic day, students have opportunities to interact with peers.

Strategy 3

Teach Formal Register and Story Structure

"Initially I came into the aha! Process meeting with Ruby Payne with a somewhat closed mind. Given my business of athletics, I just didn't think it was probably something that I really was going to be that interested in. I thought it was probably more for academics than anything else.

"And now daily I see things that pop up that we talked about in the in-service—whether it's kids not having the language they need or a conflict involving parents that needs to be resolved and we can't get by it because they don't have the ability to talk in language that gets us to a resolution. And so I think it's across the board.

"It doesn't matter whether it's in athletics or whether it's in the classroom, the topics that we've talked about in some of these seminars are a daily thing. This meeting has definitely helped me in my position."

—Eric Armstrong, High School Athletic Director

Language Resources Involve Registers of Language, Discourse Patterns, Vocabulary Development, and Story Structure

Language resources allow a person to share understandings, experiences, and information with others. Without language, the only other options are drawings or non-verbal signals. Groups of people over time also decide how to organize the language. These organizational patterns show up in stories, word choice, and discourse patterns (the organization of information in speech and writing).

Language is the tool to build social capital, to express thinking, to organize and relate personal experience. The greater the specificity of language, the cleaner and clearer the thinking can be. Eskimos, for example, have more than 15 words for snow. These words allow Eskimos to identify the subtle variations in snow because it's so important to their personal experience.

The first issue in language is the registers of language.

Registers of Language

According to linguist Martin Joos, every language in the world has five registers. These registers are the following:

Register	Explanation
Frozen	Language that is always the same. For example: Lord's Prayer, wedding vows, etc.
Formal	The standard sentence syntax and word choice of work and school. Has complete sentences and specific word choice.
Consultative	Formal register when used in conversation. Discourse pattern not quite as direct as formal register.
Casual	Language between friends and is characterized by a 400- to 800-word vocabulary. Word choice general and not specific. Conversation dependent upon non-verbal assists. Sentence syntax often incomplete.
Intimate	Language between lovers or twins. Language of sexual harassment.

RULE: Martin Joos found that one can go one register down in the same conversation, and that is socially acceptable. However, to drop two registers or more in the same conversation is to be socially offensive.

Researchers Betty Hart and Todd Risley, in their book *Meaningful Differences in the Everyday Experience of Young American Children,* found that the amount of vocabulary that children have access to prior to schooling varies significantly by the economic level of the household. Hart and Risley also discovered that the *kinds* of messages heard by children vary greatly between most welfare households and most professional households.

Research about language in children ages 1 to 4 years from stable households by economic group			
Number of words exposed to	Economic group	Affirmations (strokes)	Prohibitions (discounts)
13 million words	Welfare	1 for every	2
26 million words	Working class	2 for every	1
45 million words	Professional	6 for every	1

Source: Adapted from *Meaningful Differences in the Everyday Experience of Young American Children* by Betty Hart and Todd R. Risley.

What makes formal register so important? It is where the abstract words are. "Situated learning" theory states that one must go to the decontextualized information base to be formally schooled. Most of the decontextualized vocabulary is in formal register and uses language that is less sensory and more abstract. For example, one might say in formal register that a situation was physically violent while in casual register one would say that he hit him.

When a person doesn't have much vocabulary in formal register, then conflict resolution is an issue as well. What Roger Fisher and William Ury state in their book *Getting to YES* is that a person must go from the personal to the issue to resolve a conflict. Most of the issue words are in formal register.

Strategies to Address Formal Register in Discipline

Many students get kicked out of school primarily for being in the wrong register. When a student goes to casual or intimate register at school, we are offended because it is our expectation that students will be at the formal or consultative level. At aha! Process we teach students to translate between levels. At the elementary level we draw a picture of a newscaster for formal register and a picture of a friend for casual register. We tell students there are two ways to say everything. Then we have them restate the casual statement in formal register. At the secondary level we teach them all the registers.

Casual Register (the language of close friends)	Formal Register (the language of school and business)
Wuz zat chew say?	▪ Could you repeat that, please?
This sucks.	▪ I really don't appreciate this activity because it doesn't seem relevant to my present situation. ▪ That seems to be an injustice. ▪ Without proper preparation and/or an extension of the deadline, I do not feel capable of completing the task before me.
My bad.	▪ It was my fault. Please excuse me. ▪ I accept responsibility for my grievous error. ▪ I apologize for my *faux pas*.
Just chillin'.	▪ I'm relaxing and enjoying the company of my peers. ▪ I'm delighted to be in the solitude of my environment.
That's tight.	▪ That's cool.
That's da bomb.	▪ This activity has overwhelmed me with its superlative value and significant application to my future. ▪ This is an excellent suggestion. ▪ I would like to compliment you on your choice of …
Wuz up?	▪ How are you doing?
Me bad!	▪ I believe my performance demonstrated superior preparation and execution.
Huh?	▪ Pardon me, Mr. (or Ms.) _____, I didn't understand what you said.
… Groan …	▪ I made an error. ▪ I feel uncomfortable. ▪ I do not wish to comply with your request. Would you consider an alternative?
Hook me up.	▪ Would you be so kind as to introduce me to …? ▪ I would appreciate your assistance.

(continued on next page)

(continued from previous page)

Casual Register (the language of close friends)	Formal Register (the language of school and business)
F_____ S_____ H_____ D_____	▪ The pain is excruciating! ▪ I disagree. ▪ Would you reconsider your decision?
You dissin' me?	▪ Are you disrespecting me?

Source: Adapted from Leander (Texas) Independent School District.

1. Teach registers and how to translate. It's important for students to know that they need both casual and formal register.

2. Sometimes students will tell you that formal register is "white" or "uppity." We reply that formal register is the language of money, and you have to speak it if you want to have money.

3. Have a whole-class activity where students translate words. It can be fun—and quite enlightening! Have each student write a few paragraphs in casual register on a particular subject and then, as a group, translate to formal register. What follows is an example of an adult who was trying to translate casual into formal. *(Editor's note: All errors in the ensuing letter have been intentionally retained. As you can tell, it is badly written and makes little sense to readers with formal register.)*

> *Let me begin to inform you that we cannot express our concern for your absence in the June workshop. We understand that the difficulties that were involved in arriving were too great for some participants enrolled in this workshop. If at all possible we would have spoken with everyone to ensure a route to get there safely, but in this matter that was impossible; our apologies go out to you.*

> *This matter has forced our company to allow options for your inconvenience. Unfortunately we are not going to be able to grant permission for refunds of any type. Reason begin that we were still able to hold the workshop without any difficulties and over 180 people were able to attend the workshop without any problem. Needless to say we are not trying to state in any way that you were, indeed, not able*

to participate in the workshop because of some type of catastrophe. There are many reasons why an individual could not have attended the workshop, but on the same note if our office were to go and identify and handle each situation differently than we would be handling this for days maybe weeks. Not to say that you are not worth are time, because you are. The options that we are offering are fair and quite manageable to everyone who unfortunately could not attend this workshop.

Option 1 is going to be attending the workshop that we have coming up in October. Option 2 is going to be attending the workshop we have coming up in December. Payment can be transferred in full to either workshop because of the circumstances that lie. When you make your decision, please call _____ and speak to _____ and I will get you all squared up as you need to be. If the options are not what you would consider fair, than please feel free to call and express your case at the same above number and speak, once again, to me and we will see what we can do for your situation. Thank you very much and I'll be waiting to here back from you.

Formal register in writing and speaking is an entrée into the job market. It is truly the language of money and is necessary for understanding textbooks, written texts, business letters, etc.

Patterns of Discourse

In the oral-language tradition in which the casual register operates, the pattern of discourse is quite different. (Discourse is defined as the organizational pattern of information.) First, however, we look at the discourse pattern of formal register.

Formal-Register Discourse Pattern

Speaker or writer gets straight to the point.

Casual-Register Discourse Pattern

Writer or speaker goes around the issue before finally coming to the point.

Strategies to Develop Discourse Patterns

1. One of the best tools for developing discourse patterns is through writing. Mental models of organizational patterns can be taught and used to structure one's writing.

These mental models show students that text uses different organizational structures to convey information.

2. Teach students how to go through non-fiction text systematically using this process. Here are the steps for each text passage.
   a. Box in titles and subtitles.
   b. Trace paragraphs and number them.
   c. Read the paragraph and, at the end of the paragraph, write ST, which means *Stop* and *Think*.
   d. Go back through each paragraph and circle no more than two words that give a general idea of what that paragraph is about.
   e. Write a brief summary of each paragraph.

f. Draw a mental model of the main ideas.

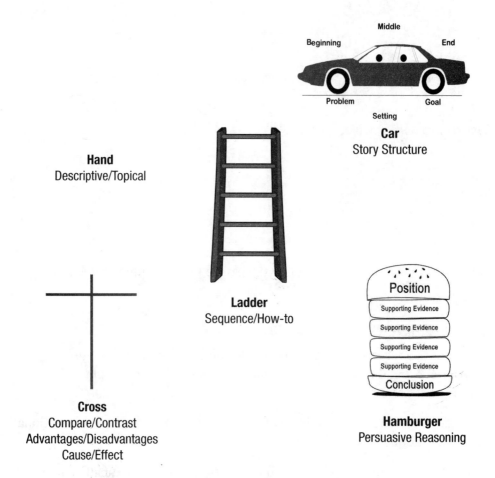

Diet During Pregnancy Could Have Effects That Last to Adulthood

by Sharon Begley

As mysteries go, these don't seem to have much in common: A child born underweight has a higher than normal risk of developing heart disease, diabetes, obesity and hypertension as an adult. One identical twin develops schizophrenia, which studies of families show is a genetic disease, but the other twin is spared.

Last week's column looked at scientists' growing realization that, when it comes to important changes in the genome—if I may corrupt an old political mantra— "It's not just the sequence, stupid." Mice with identical genes for fur color may be brownish or yellow, depending on whether their gene for fur color has been silenced by what their mother ate during pregnancy. It's beginning to look as if such "epigenetic" changes, defined as those having no effect on the sequence of molecules that make up a genome, may be major players in determining traits and disease risk.

"The completion of the human genome project is a monumental event, but there's still an enormous amount that we have not yet fleshed out," says psychiatrist James Potash of Johns Hopkins University School of Medicine, Baltimore. "Epigenetic variation is one."

Take the enigma of fetal programming, in which nutrition during gestation seems to affect the risk of disease decades later. At a June conference on the subject, attended by some 700 scientists, "What came shining through is that birth weight affects the risk of diabetes, coronary heart disease, obesity, hypertension and breast or prostate cancers," says David Barker of England's University of Southampton. Scrawny newborns, in general, grow up to have a higher incidence of the first four; chubby ones, a higher risk of the latter.

At first, scientists thought the reason was physiology, not genetics. For example, newborns who are small for their length probably have fewer kidney cells than they should. Since the kidneys regulate blood pressure, undersized kidneys can increase later risk of hypertension and thus heart disease, explains Dr. Barker.

But fetal programming "almost certainly" reflects epigenetic changes, too, says Craig Cooney of the University of Arkansas for Medical Sciences. That's because, much as in the mice whose color reflects what mom ate while pregnant, nutrients reaching the human fetus can include more or fewer of the molecules that silence or activate genes. Maybe too few nutrients during gestation might mean not enough of the molecules that silence heart-disease-causing genes.

"The nutrition an embryo receives at crucial states of development can have important and lasting effects on the expression of various genes, including those involved in health and disease," says Randy Jirtle of Duke University Medical Center, Durham, N.C.

One target of such silencing must have Gregor Mendel turning over in his grave. The Austrian monk, regarded as the founder of genetics, concluded that which parent a gene comes from is irrelevant. True, we carry two copies of every gene (except those on the Y chromosome), one from mom and one from dad. But dozens of genes in sperm or ova are tagged with the biochemical equivalent of "don't mind me." Throughout life, those genes are silenced, or "imprinted." If mom's gene is imprinted, only dad's counts; if dad's is imprinted, only mom's counts.

The gene sequence hasn't changed, so imprinting is epigenetic— and something you don't want to mess up. When the gene for insulin-like growth factor 2 (IGF2) loses its imprinting, for instance, the once-silenced copy is activated, loosing a flood of growth factor that promotes childhood and adult cancers. Yet if you were to sequence that IGF2 gene, it would look just fine.

Such imprinting mistakes may be affecting some test-tube babies. The incidence of a rare genetic disease called Beckwith-Wiedemann syndrome was six times as high as in children conceived the traditional way, according to a study published in January. This syndrome occurs when IGF2 loses its "keep quiet" marker.

"There is reason to believe, from animal studies, that assisted-reproductive technology can lead to more frequent imprinting errors," says Hopkins geneticist Andrew Feinberg. One suspect: the broth in which ova and embryos grow before being implanted in the mother's womb. It may somehow unsilence imprinted genes.

Epigenetics might also solve the puzzle of identical twins who do not have the same "genetic" diseases, especially psychiatric ones. "You wonder if the difference might be that something causes a gene related to mental illness to be silenced in one twin but not the other," says Dr. Potash.

In the old joke, a drunk searches for his lost keys under a streetlight, not because he dropped them there, but because the light is good. The search for genetic variants—the differences in DNA sequences—underlying complex diseases is starting to look like that. Sequence variants are easy to find; the light's good there, so scientists have found more than a million sequence variants. But they don't correspond too well with genetically based complex diseases. No wonder the spotlight is turning from genetics to epigenetics, the pattern of gene silencing and activation.

Here is an example:

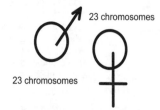

23 chromosomes

23 chromosomes

1. Fertilization

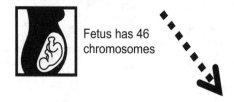

Fetus has 46 chromosomes

2. Nutrition

4. Determines diseases and traits

3. Silenced   Activated

OR

Activated   Silenced

Nutrients can either be

imprinted   activated

(silent)

G
E
N
E
S

Vocabulary Development

Vocabulary development is essential to thinking and shared understandings. Vocabulary is developed in part by knowing how things are alike and how they are different. It's easier to identify differences than it is to identify similarities. Here are two strategies for vocabulary development.

#1 Knowledge Ratings

Using a graph like the one below, have students list the words in the first column to be studied. They evaluate their knowledge level of each word and check the appropriate box. If they have some idea of the meaning, they write in their guess. Following discussion or study, they write the definition in their own words. This activity is particularly useful in helping students develop metacognitive (being able to think about one's own thinking) awareness.

Example

Word	Know	Think i know	Have heard	Guess	Definition
saline			X	A liquid for contact lenses	A salt solution

Activity

Word	Know	Think i know	Have heard	Guess	Definition
torsade					
lurdane					
macula					

#2 Word Web

Students write the target word in the box, then write a synonym, an antonym, a definition, and an experience to complete the web.

Example

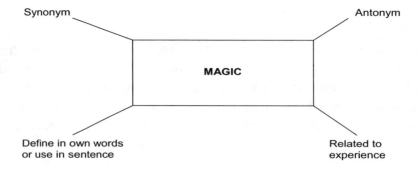

Activity

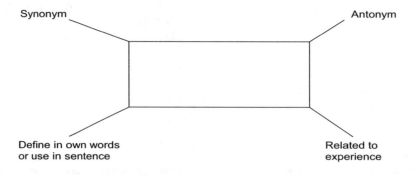

Story Structure

The way personal experience is organized in words is usually through a story. There is more than one way to organize a story. When the story is in writing, it usually follows the formal story structure pattern. (Exceptions are the use of flashback, foreshadowing, etc.) But when a story is told orally, often the end is told first. When people gossip, they tell the end first and then fill in the details.

Formal-Register Story Structure

The *formal-register story structure* starts at the beginning of the story and goes to the end in a chronological or accepted narrative pattern. The most important part of the story is the plot.

Casual-Register Story Structure

The *casual-register story structure* begins with the end of the story first or the part with the greatest emotional intensity. The story is told in vignettes, with audience participation in between. The story ends with a comment about the character and the character's value. The most important part of the story is the characterization.

What strategies work with both story structures?

It is very important that both story structures be used. The formal-register story structure most often shows up in writing and is what is tested on state assessments. The casual-register story structure has the richness of character development.

Two strategies help develop both.

Have a student tell a story two times. The first time the student tells the story you listen. Then you have the student to tell it a second time; you ask questions and take notes. The third time *you* tell the story from the notes, and the student will tell you whether it's correct or not.

Show the students the two drawings on page 50 and tell them there are two ways to tell a story: one is the way you tell it to your friends, while the other is the way you might tell it in a textbook. Organize students into groups of five or six and have them read a story in a book. On paper they draw the main characters and the main events. Have them stand in front of the class and retell the story the way it is in the book. Then have the student with the end of the story get in front of the line, have the rest of the students mix up however they wish, and have them tell the story as they would to a friend. While they tell it, the class throws in comments about how they feel about the characters and the events.

Language—how we structure it and the words we use—determines our ability to communicate beyond ourselves with a wider audience. Vocabulary can limit *or enhance* both experience and the development of social capital as much as any other factor. The gift of language is unparalleled; it is the gift of thinking itself.

Steps to Follow

1. Have students translate language from casual to formal.

2. Teach in formal register, explain concepts in consultative register, and build relationships in consultative language.

3. Use graphic organizers to teach formal patterns of story structure and written text.

4. Teach students phrases to resolve conflict; such phrases often come from formal register.

5. Teach the vocabulary of the content as it is in formal register.

Strategy 4

Teach Tools for Negotiating the Abstract Representational World

Most of the approaches to teaching and learning address issues of instruction or the teaching part. This chapter is going to look at the learning part. In other words, what must students do inside their heads to learn—and then be able to use the information?

In order to survive in school, a learner must be able to negotiate the abstract representational world, which is the paper world or the world as represented on a computer screen. This takes a different skill set because of the requirement that sensory information be represented on paper. For example, an apple in three dimensions does not look like a two-dimensional drawing of an apple. The drawing only represents the apple on paper. Words represent a feeling, but they are not the feeling. A photo represents a person, but it is not the person. Numbers represent an amount, but they are not the actual item being counted.

What Is the Paper World?

The paper world is how information and understandings are conveyed in formal schooling. Words, symbols, etc., are used to convey the meaning. Paper does not have non-verbals, emotions, or human interaction. Paper depends on a shared understanding of vocabulary in order to communicate. If you grew up in a household where there were very few books, calendars, clocks, etc., the concept of information on paper is difficult. It has to be learned.

Abstract, decontextualized, representational symbols, ideas, etc., are on paper to represent a tangible, sensory reality. Here are some examples:

Abstract item	Represents
Grades	The ticket to get into college, a better job, more money
House deed	The physical property
Address	The physical location
Social Security number	The person (way to keep track of people on paper)
Daily to-do list	Daily tasks
Clock or calendar	Abstract time
State assessment	Knowledge base and personal vocabulary; a representation of shared understandings for communication
Homework	Ability to complete a task in a given time frame, to prove understandings
Insurance papers	An external support system that provides money, assistance, and expertise for unusual circumstances, health, etc.
Driver's license	The right to physically drive a vehicle
TV guide	The shows
Photograph	The person (a photo doesn't breathe; it's a two-dimensional representation of the person)
Letters in alphabet	Symbols that represent a physical sound
Numbers	Symbols that represent quantity
Musical notations	Symbols that represent sounds and timing
Road map	Objects, roads, etc., in physical space
Sonogram	A three-dimensional representation of an object
MRI (magnetic resonance imaging)	A three-dimensional representation of a body, body part, etc. (it isn't the body, but it represents the body)
Trust document	A legal entity (has its own Social Security number) that pays taxes, owns property, and identifies how assets will be held and distributed over time
Student handbook	Paper version of the appropriate behaviors that are to be used
Teacher contract	A legal document that establishes expectations for teachers' compensation, benefits, terms of employment, etc.
Menu	The food choices in a restaurant (it isn't the food itself)

Continuum of Paper Documents

As your financial situation increases and grows, the amount of paper documents in a household indicates to some extent your familiarity and comfort with the paper world.

birth certificates
immunization records
driver's license
rental agreements
money orders
paycheck stubs
bills

wills
magazines/newspapers
payment records
credit-card and bank
  statements
mortgage papers
calendars
planners
to-do lists
tax returns
books
coupons
passports

corporate financial statements
prenuptial agreement
stock certificates/personal
  investments
provenance
property deeds
charity events/invitations
board of directors minutes/records
club memberships
trusts

In their research on situated learning, Brown, Collins, and Duguid reveal how

different schooling is from the activities and culture that give meaning and purpose to what students learn elsewhere … Lave and Wenger focus on the behavior of JPFs (just plain folks) and record that the ways they learn are quite distinct from what students are asked to do (page 27).

	Just plain folks	Student	Practicing individual or apprentice
Reason with	Causal stories	Laws	Causal models
Act on	Situations	Symbols	Conceptual situations
Resolve	Emergent problems and dilemmas	Well-defined problems	Ill-defined problems
Produce	Negotiable meaning and socially constructed understanding	Fixed meaning and immutable concepts	Negotiable meaning and socially constructed understanding

Source: "Situated Cognition and the Culture of Learning" by John Seely Brown, Allan Collins, and Paul Duguid. *Educational Researcher.* Vol. 18, No. 1. January-February 1989. pages 32–42.

Situated-learning research further indicates that the learning occurs in a context within a set of relationships and cultural norms. Lave and Wenger's *Situated Learning* states that for newcomers to the group "the purpose is not to learn *from* talk as a substitute for legitimate peripheral participation; it is to learn *to* talk as a key to legitimate peripheral participation" (pages 108–109). Wenger's *Communities of Practice* also says that this participation creates a shared repertoire of communal resources, which Wenger defines as routines, behaviors, vocabulary, etc.

In other words, hidden rules come out of the environment and are situated in context, culture, and relationships. Furthermore, in the situated-learning approach, learning is always contextualized and relationship-based. School learning, on the other hand, is decontextualized and abstract (on paper, devoid of immediate relationships, using generalized representations).

What Are the Hidden Rules of Learning at School, i.e., the Decontextualized Environment?

Hidden Rules of Learning at School

"Situated" learning in an environment where there is not much formal schooling	Formal school learning environment
Language is oral and uses many non-verbals.	Language is written, with specific word choice and sentence structure.
Math skills are related to trading, bartering, specific tasks, money.	Math tasks/skills are written and involve generic, unrelated story problems, formulas, and patterns.
Teaching/learning is very relational; respect may or may not be given to the learning and/or teaching.	The relationship between teacher and learner is much more formalized; respect is expected by the teacher from the learner.
Learning environment is often unpredictable; reactive skills are important.	Planning is required in formal learning; both teacher and learner are expected to be able to plan.
Information is conveyed through story or media.	Information is conveyed through textbook and/or lecture.
Laughter is used to lessen conflict.	Laughter during conflict is viewed as disrespectful.
Paper (decontextualized) information is not valued.	Decontextualized information is what is tested and valued.

What Do We Know About Beginning Learning in a Decontextualized Environment?

The school learning environment for the most part is "decontextualized" from the situation and relationships. When learning becomes decontextualized, then the amount of supports a student needs to transfer to that environment increase.

Teaching is outside the head and the body; learning is inside the head and the body.

To begin our discussion, a distinction will be made between the brain and the mind. Truth be told, it is all one and the same. But for the purposes of this chapter, the brain is going to mean what you inherited, and the mind will be what was developed by your environment. Cognitive scientists have concluded that it's about a 50/50 arrangement. About half of whom an individual becomes is developed by genetic code and about half by environment.

All functions of the brain are either a chemical or electrical interaction. A chemical interaction occurs on the face of the cell and continues down the tail (axon) of the cell as an electrical impulse. When the electrical impulse enters the dendrites and synapses, causing their structure to permanently change, learning has occurred. Therefore, learning is physiological. That's why it takes so long to "unlearn" something that has been learned incorrectly.

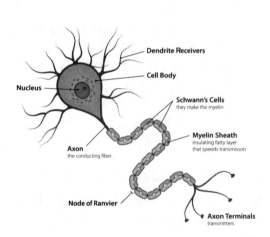

Chemicals in the brain come from four sources: what the genetic code indicates will be made, hormonal fluctuations, external experience (you get frightened and produce adrenaline), and what you eat and breathe.

What is the mind as it's being defined here? It is the part that was learned in the environment. But more importantly, it is the abstract replication/representation of external reality. What does that mean?

As human beings, we are very limited. We cannot communicate telepathically. Wouldn't it be nice if we could communicate by, say, rubbing heads? Well, we can't. So we use abstract representational systems, which illustrate common understandings, in order to communicate. Numbers, language, drawings, etc. … all are forms of this.

For example, in the winter, "cold" is measured by a thermometer. However, the sensory reality of cold is not the same as the measured reality of cold. After the temperature gets 10 below zero, it's hard to tell the difference between 10 below zero and 40 below zero. Both are cold. The measurement system is the abstract overlay of the sensory-based reality.

How did we get this abstract structure? We got it from the interplay of language and experience in our environment. When we were young, we were mediated by the adults in our life. What they did when they mediated us was to give us the what, the why, and the how. In other words, they pointed out the stimulus (what we were to pay attention to), gave it meaning (the why), and gave us a strategy (how).

Mediation

Point out the stimulus (*what*)	Give it meaning (*why*)	Provide a strategy (*how*)

For example, a parent says to a child:

- "Don't cross the street without looking" (*what*).
- "You could be killed" (*why*).
- "Look both ways twice before you cross the street" (*how*).

This mediation builds an abstract architecture inside the child's head. That architecture acts as an abstract replication of external reality, just as the blueprint acts as an abstract replication of a house.

Mediation is particularly required when an individual is a new learner to a skill, process, content … whatever.

Research on new learners (Benjamin Bloom and D. C. Berliner) indicates that there is a process that an individual goes through on the path toward mental acuity.

Novice	Has no experience with information, skill, process, etc. Needs terminology, models, and procedures. Needs context-free rules.
Advanced beginner	Has some experience and begins to collect episodic knowledge (stories) and strategic knowledge (strategies). Begins to see similarities across contexts and situations.
Competent	Can make conscious choices about what will and will not work. Can distinguish important from unimportant. Takes personal responsibility for own learning because of knowing what actions made a difference.
Proficient	Sees hundreds of patterns and sorts information quickly by pattern. Uses intuition and know-how to make judgments. Has wealth of experience from which to make generalizations and judgments.
Expert	Makes own rules because of extensive experience. Performance is so fluid it can happen virtually without conscious thought; this is called automaticity.

A beginning learner in anything needs the three components of mediation—the what, the why, and the how. Often experts have difficulty helping a novice because so many of the experts' actions are at the level of automaticity, and the experts have a great deal of difficulty articulating what they are doing. This dynamic is frequently seen in sports.

There is a rule in cognitive research that goes like this:

The more complex the process an individual is involved in, the more parts of that process need to be at the level of automaticity.

For example, when a child learns to ride a bicycle, training wheels are often used. But a skilled rider would never use training wheels. What the training wheels allow the child to do is learn to steer, guide, pedal, and brake. When those are more at the level of automaticity, then the training wheels are taken off, and additional skills are developed.

So it's a mistake to teach beginners in the same way one would teach a skilled individual.

Second, the brain processes things differently when one is a new learner.

In the book *Making Connections* by Renate Nummela Caine and Geoffrey Caine, the authors describe two different kinds of memory functions in the brain. One is used by beginning learners (taxon), while the other is used by individuals who have more experience with it (locale).

Taxon	Locale
No context (experience)	Context (experience)
Memory capacity: about five things	Unlimited memory
Requires continuous rehearsal to remember	Remembers quickly but has loss of accessibility over period of time
Is in short-term memory	Is in long-term memory
Limited to extrinsic motivation	Motivated by novelty, curiosity, expectation (intrinsic)
Specific, habit-like behaviors that are resistant to change	Updated continuously, flexible
Isolated items	Interconnected, spatial memory
Not connected to meaning	Has meaning that is motivated by need to make sense
Acquisition of relatively fixed routes	Forms initial maps quickly and involves sensory activity and emotion; generates personal maps through creation of personal meaning
Follows route	Uses map

What this means is that a beginning learner must be mediated in order to learn. Beginners must be given the what, the why, and the how.

Often in schools, the focus is on the content; the why and how are seldom if ever mentioned, so the student is unable to do the work.

Abstract Representational Systems

One of the reasons you and I are successful is that we have been mediated, not only in sensory data, but also in abstract data. What does that mean?

Just as a computer has icons to represent the software, so does the mind.

What are these abstractions or representations?

A few summers ago it was so hot in Fort Worth, Texas, that the railroad tracks warped. We keep butter out in our house, and it kept melting. One day I said to a friend, "The thermometer says it's 72 degrees in here, but the butter is melting. In the winter, it says 72 degrees and the butter doesn't melt." My friend said, "Don't confuse real heat with measured heat."

You see, Anders Celsius and Gabriel Fahrenheit decided they wanted a better way to talk about heat, so each designed a system to do so. But the systems are abstract representations and measurements of a sensory-based reality.

Language is the tool we use to create and acknowledge those abstract systems. Abstract systems are learned. If a student comes from an environment where there is heavy reliance on casual register, and there isn't much formal education, often the student has few abstract representational systems.

Furthermore, abstractions are stored in the mind in either visual or auditory rhythmic memory. Abstractions are kept in mental models. **Mental models are in the form of a story, a metaphor, an analogy—or, perhaps, a two-dimensional drawing.**

For example, when a house is being built, blueprints are used. The blueprints become the abstract representational system for the final sensory-based object, the house.

Another example: A lawyer I know got a call from a colleague who was in court and needed a piece of paper from his desk. She said, "Your desk is a mess. No one could find it." And he said to her, "Go stand in front of my desk. Picture an overlay of a map of the United States. That paper is somewhere around Vermont." And she found it. He had given her an abstract representational system.

What Are the Key Issues in Transition to a Paper World (Abstract Representational World)?

If you are an individual who has mostly grown up in a situated-learning environment, how do you make the transition to the decontextualized world of school?

The first transition is understanding how ideas get presented on paper. For example, decoding in reading is simply assigning a sound to a set of symbols. *Sh* represents a sound. One of the fastest ways to move individuals from a sensory reality to a representational paper world is to use mental models.

The First Key Issue Is Mental Models

1. **Mental models are how the mind holds abstract information, i.e., information that has no sensory representation.**

   Each of us carries much abstract information around in our head every day. How do we do this? We carry it in mental models.

   Just as a computer has a file manager to represent the structure of the software content, so does the human mind.

2. **All subject areas or disciplines have their own blueprints or mental models.**

   In other words, they have their own way to structure information. For two people to communicate, there must be shared understanding.

   This shared understanding comes from the study of subject matter. All occupations and all disciplines have their own mental models. To communicate about that occupation or discipline, an understanding of those mental models (abstract blueprints) is necessary.

3. **Mental models tell us what is and is not important in the discipline. They help the mind sort.**

4. **Mental models often explain "the why" of things working the way they do.**

5. **Mental models tell the structure, purpose, process, or pattern.**

   That's how the mind sorts what is and is not important. The mind can remember only when it can "chunk" and sort information.

6. **Mental models are held in the mind as stories, analogies, or two-dimensional drawings.**

7. **Mental models "collapse" the amount of time it takes to teach and learn something.**

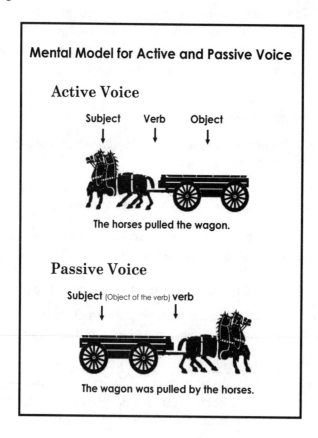

8. Mental models of a discipline are contained within the units of the curriculum.

To illustrate, math is about assigning order and value to the universe. We tend to assign order and value in one of three ways: numbers, space, and time. Fractions, for example, are a part of math curricula because fractions are the shared understanding of part to whole of *space*. Decimals are studied because decimals tell part to whole of *numbers*.

Lee Shulman found in his research that the difference between a good and excellent teacher is the depth of understanding the latter has of the discipline.

What are examples of mental models? Teachers have used them forever. But, too often, educators haven't found ways to share them with other teachers. They are the drawings, the verbal stories, the analogies that are given as part of instruction. As one teacher said, "It is how I explain it."

Content is organized by the constructs of the disciplines (or the mental models). Here are some examples.

Content	Purpose
Language Arts	Using structure and language to communicate
Math	Assigning order and value to the universe
Biology	Identifying living systems and relationships within and among those systems
Chemistry	Bonding
Algebra	Solving for the unknown through functions
Geometry	Using logic to order and assign values to form and space
Physics	Using matter and energy through math applications
Social Studies	Identifying patterns of people and governments over time
Earth Science	Identifying and predicting physical phenomena

For example, because Language Arts is about using structure and language to communicate, virtually all Language Arts curriculum at the secondary level is divided by genres, i.e., poetry, drama, grammar, etc. Those curricular divisions end up reflecting the structures of the various disciplines.

For example, the purpose of Chemistry is bonding. The structure where the bonding occurs is a theoretical construct (shell theory, now string theory). The reason the periodic table is used is because it represents patterns of bonding. Equations are used because they provide the process by which the bonding is calculated.

9. There are generic mental models.

In addition to having mental models for subject areas or disciplines, there also are mental models for occupations. To be successful in work or school one must have four generic mental models. They are: space, time, part to whole, and formal register. These mental models are basic to all tasks.

Space

Space becomes important because your body operates in space. The mind must have a way to keep track of your body. One way is to touch everything. Another way is to assign a reference system to space using abstract words and drawings. For example, we talk about east, west, north, south, up, down, etc. Because math is about assigning order and value to the universe, we tend to do it directionally. Another illustration: We write small to large numbers from left to right. To read a map, one must have a reference for space. To find things in your office or desk, there must be an abstract referencing system for space.

Time

A mental model for abstract time (days, minutes, weeks, hours, etc.) is crucial to success in school and work. One way to keep time is emotionally (how it feels), but another is abstractly with a calendar or a clock. Past, present, and future must be in the mental model because, without these, it isn't possible to sequence.

If you cannot sequence, then …	You cannot plan.
If you cannot plan, then …	You cannot predict.
If you cannot predict, then …	You cannot identify cause and effect.
If you cannot identify cause and effect, then …	You cannot identify consequence.
If you cannot identify consequence, then …	You cannot control impulsivity.
If you cannot control impulsivity, then …	You have an inclination toward criminal behavior.

Source: Adapted from work of Reuven Feuerstein.

Examples of a mental model for time would be a timeline, calendar, schedule, or clock.

Part to Whole

Part to whole means that one can identify the parts, as well as the whole. For example, chapters make a book. Words make a sentence. You cannot effectively analyze anything unless you can break it down and understand part to whole.

Formal Register

Because formal register is the language currency of work and school, it becomes crucial to have an understanding of it.

10. **Sketching is a technique that can be used in the classroom to identify each student's mental models.**
    Simply ask students to sketch (draw in two dimensions) what a word or concept means to them. If they cannot sketch anything, it probably isn't inside their head.

The Second Key Issue Is Vocabulary—or the *'What'*

Vocabulary becomes the tool by which the mind categorizes information (like and different), sorts the information, assigns the information to a pattern or group, and then communicates shared meaning. One of the misunderstandings of constructivism was that as long as students made meaning inside their heads, they were OK. But meaning only has value to the extent that it can be shared and communicated. This requires a shared understanding of what a word means. Vocabulary literally is the key tool for thinking.

One of the reasons so many secondary students have trouble with Algebra is that Algebra is the course where one goes from sensory math to abstract representational math. The vocabulary alone keeps many students from succeeding.

Here is an example of how to teach math vocabulary using a mental model.

The Third Key Issue Is Direct-Teaching the Processes—or the 'How'

To do any task requires a *"how"* component that is the process. Unless the how is directly taught, a student does not have a tool to complete the task. One of the reasons generic study skills have not been as successful as the researchers would like is that processes are specific to tasks.

For example, a technique for doing research appears on the next page.

Each student takes a manila folder and glues six envelopes to the inside of it. Each envelope is a topic that will be researched. For example, if the report is on an animal, one envelope would be for habitat, one for habits, etc. One envelope is for the bibliography cards. On the outside of each envelope is written 4, 3, 2, 1 (or the number of 3x5 cards that the students need to find about that topic). As the students completes a 3x5 card, they put it in the appropriate envelope and then cross off a number. If there is not a bibliography card made for that source, then one is made and put in that envelope also. When the students are ready to write, they pull the cards out of the envelope and write the paper.

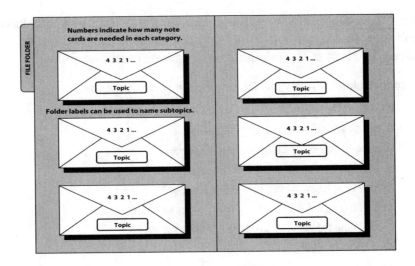

The Fourth Key Issue Is Having the Students Develop Questions

Question making has a huge payoff in learning. Question making is the tool that allows you to get inside your brain and know what you know and what you don't know. When students say to you, "I don't understand," and you ask them what part they don't understand, and they say, "All of it," then you know the student doesn't know how to ask questions syntactically. Anne Marie Palincsar found in her research that if you cannot ask questions, you rarely get past the third-grade reading level. So it can be taught.

> *"I think the most beneficial strategy I have used in the classroom has been question making. At our middle school we have a semester-long competition playing 'Jeopardy!' The students have really enjoyed it, and they have actually gotten into writing their own questions. It has paid off in terms of their comprehension. Also, I have extensively used mental models ... This strategy really enables the students to connect some of the things they're learning and remember material so much easier. In this way they can really make it their own knowledge."*
>
> –Brian Conner, Middle School Science Teacher

A quick approach is to give students the question stems and then have them use the rules to develop a multiple-choice question. Creating multiple-choice questions develops critical-thinking skills. Some examples follow:

Question-Making Stems (from Texas Assessment of Academic Skills)

1. What does the word _____ mean?
2. What can you tell from the following passage?
3. What does the author give you reason to believe?
4. What is the best summary of this passage?
5. Which of the following is a fact in this passage?
6. What is the main idea of the _____ paragraph?
7. Which of the following is an opinion in this passage?
8. What happens after _____?
9. How did _____ feel when _____?
10. What is the main idea of this passage?
11. Which of these happened (first/last) in the passage?
12. Which of these is not a fact in the passage?
13. Where was _____?
14. When did _____?
15. What happens when _____?
16. What was the main reason for the following _____?
17. After _____, what could _____?
18. Where does the _____ take place?
19. Which of these best describes _____ before/after _____?

More Question-Making Stems

1. From this passage (story), how might _____ be described?
2. Why was _____?
3. Why did _____?
4. How else might the author have ended the passage (story)?
5. If the author had been _____, how might the information have been different?
6. In this passage, what does _____ mean?
7. How did _____ feel about _____?
8. What caused _____ to _____?
9. What is _____?
10. When _____ happened, why did _____?
11. The passage states that _____.
12. Why is that information important to the reader?

The key process to educate now is autonomous and competitive.

It needs to change to be relational learning.

The Fifth Key Issue Is Relational Learning

What is relational learning? It is when the learning occurs in a context of mutual respect and the student has a group to which the student belongs for learning. This becomes a support system.

When adults are learning something new, rarely do they make the learning autonomous and competitive. For example, several years ago I went to Europe for the first time with a friend. Neither of us had been to Europe. So we learned together. We didn't say, *OK, let's make this trip a competition and see who does the best and then we'll grade ourselves and see who has the best grade!* No, we relied on each other to make it through the trip.

All learning occurs within a social context and relationship and has since the beginning of time. People in the school business have tried very hard to make learning a separate endeavor from relationships. The students who succeed in school have the ability to establish relationships and belong to a group. Why not create the processes so they are available to all students?!

In addition, many of the students who fail do not have a support system, i.e., adults and resources outside the school system that provide the support to succeed in school. Mentors and social-media contacts with outside sources are two ways to do that. (Please review Strategy 2 for more on relational learning.)

If staff availability and the time to learn (schedule) are the constants, and the only process for learning is autonomous and competitive, then learning becomes the variable.

If learning is the constant, then content availability (in any time frame) becomes the variable, and the process for learning becomes relational.

At the Secondary Level, the Sixth Key Issue Is Content Availability

The **purpose of public schooling** in the United States is to provide education for *everyone* in a given geographic area through the age of 18 to your 19th birthday; the student cannot be charged a fee for basic education.

Given that mandate, what structure would allow that to happen? In other words, how do you structure the institution so that you can achieve that purpose? For a while we used the concept of the one-room school. But then we had too many children. So we went to the German graded-school concept, which we are now using.

Secondary schools are structured against the schedule, the courses that the state says they must offer, the number of students they have, and the availability of staff. The first thing into the schedule are the singletons (courses offered only once during the day—either because of the demands of the course (e.g., Band), the number of students taking the course (e.g., Advanced Placement Calculus), or athletics. The athletic program in virtually every secondary school is scheduled first because of the amount of public attention to the quality of the program and the amount of support that comes from the community for the athletic program. Then the number of sections of a required course are figured into the schedule.

The three other major structures that determine the schedule are the facility, the money, and the law. Limited facilities are particularly problematic for scheduling Physical Education, lunch, and specialty subjects (labs, courses that require specialized equipment, etc.). Money always is a structure because the number of staff persons a school is allowed to have is based upon FTE (full-time equivalent, i.e., the number of full-time staff allowed). The law (a combination of federal law, state law, school board policy, and union agreements) says what must be offered to the student, that teachers must have a 30-minute, duty-free lunch, etc.

What are the patterns that arise out of those structures? Because of student selection of given courses, the pathway through the day is heavily dictated. For example, if a student has two singletons, e.g., Band and AP Calculus (because those two courses in many secondary schools are only offered once during the day), that student will tend to be in the same classes with these same students during the day.

Further, if a ninth-grader fails two classes that year, because of the scheduling issues and course prerequisites, such a student can almost never make up the courses unless the student goes to summer school—for which most schools charge. And if you are poor or have to work, you cannot go to summer school.

For example, in the state of Texas a student must have 24 credits to graduate from high school, and the state dictates that students must have 4 credits of English, 4 of Math, etc. Ninth-graders who fail English I and Algebra I cannot go on to English II or Algebra II until they have that credit. Most high schools have a seven-period day. It takes a six-period day (6 credits each year) for four years just to get 24 credits. If you are on a seven-period day, that means you have only four extra time frames (in four years) to make up for courses that you failed.

So if in your first year you fail two courses, then you must repeat those two the next year before you can go on to the next level. And your ability to get those courses knocks you out of other courses you need because you are in a distribution pattern against the schedule. If you fail any courses your sophomore year and you can't go to summer school, you may as well drop out because you cannot finish within the given schedule.

What are the processes that result? First of all, when a student is failing or doing poorly, typically that isn't caught at all until the first grading period—and typically no interventions are done until after first semester when the grades come in. Then the counselor composes a list of who failed first semester and gives it to the principal or dean or department chairs. Typically, however, few interventions are made until the end of the school year.

How Can This Be Changed to Benefit Students?

Just change the processes and the scheduling. That would change the patterns.

It's quite simple really. If the scheduling were changed to make content available at any time during or out of the school day and the processes were changed, then the patterns would change.

> **Right now most content availability is based on staff and schedule availability. Thanks to technology, content availability can be at any time.**

Most teaching is based upon the construct that the student is already familiar with the paper world. But a student who is under-resourced may not have that familiarity. To facilitate that transition, students must have the what, the why, and the how direct-taught in a relational learning environment. Additionally, they must have multiple opportunities to visit/revisit the content.

Steps to Follow

1. Make sure students have a visual representation for each new vocabulary word. Have students "sketch" the word in a simple visual drawing. If students cannot sketch it, they probably doesn't know it.

2. Have 20% of the grade based on the process, the *"how"* of the work, and 80% on the *"what"*—i.e., the content.

3. Provide mental models (drawings, stories, analogies) so that students can connect the new concept/content with something they already know.

4. Have students construct their own mental models. It is a lifelong skill.

5. Always provide a process, or a *"how"* piece, for every assignment given.

6. Provide the tools to deal with abstract time. In other words, time and task are always linked. To complete tasks, it's very important to be able to do it in a time frame. That is a learned skill.

7. Provide alternative methods (mp3 recordings, for example) for students to revisit the information and learn it.

Strategy ⑤

Teach Appropriate Behaviors and Procedures

Build emotional resources; have a process for addressing biochemical issues

"Our failure rate has continued to decline. Six, seven, eight years ago about 11% of all the grades we gave were F's, and now we're down in the 3–4% range, so there's been a very definite improvement in the area of kids passing classes. Which leads to improved graduation rates, lower dropout rates, as well as a huge decrease in discipline referrals. Again, about eight years ago, we were doing around 1400 a year. The year we just finished we were down to about 250. A lot of different factors were in play there but definitely there were some increases in positive things we want to see."

–Ronn Roehn, High School Principal

"Mutual respect in the classroom has had a positive effect that just happened this week. I had a child who had severe emotional problems and medical issues as well. This child at the beginning of the year was hard to be around: The other kids reacted to him, he reacted to the other kids; it wasn't a pleasant thing. After we addressed some of the medical issues and put in more learning structures for this child, the other students in the class started to see the respect between the two of us grow. As that happened, the other students started to emulate that respect back toward him as well.

"I have a cookout at the end of the year. And it's for students who don't have to sign for negative behavior, and the student with severe emotional problems had already lost that privilege at the beginning of the year. One of the students in the class who is sometimes known as a bully approached me and asked if this child could possibly come to the cookout because he and his friends had noticed such a dramatic change in this boy. And it was truly an aha! moment because it was just so out of character for the boy who approached me. It was a neat experience, watching the positive respect grow in the classroom."

–Kelly Sharp, Sixth-Grade Language Arts/Social Studies Teacher

What Must You Have for a Safe Environment?

These components must be in place:

1. Relationships of mutual respect with students

In the chapter on relationships earlier in this book, mutual respect is discussed. The reality is that it is earned, taught, insisted upon, and reciprocated. It is a very difficult concept for beginning teachers to understand because it isn't about friendship. It's about being the adult, caring for the student as a human being, and insisting upon learning and appropriate behavior. Mutual respect is the bedrock of any strong discipline program.

2. A systems approach in the classroom and on the campus

Neither classroom nor campus can act independently of each other. If teachers are forced to operate independently from the campus because there's weak administration, then chaos in the building is normal.

A systems component involves these aspects, and there is a clear understanding of them.

3. Administration support

Part of the role of a school's top administrator is to provide a safe and orderly environment so that teaching and learning can occur. To do that, the administrator must:

- Establish a clear understanding and mutual respect with parents.
- Secure the support of administrator's own supervisor.
- Identify appropriate teacher behaviors and interventions.
- Provide a separate place/time for students who are harmful/disruptive to the orderly environment.
- Establish student norms for the campus.
- Ensure that the legal and ethical rights of students and teachers are enforced.
- Identify and follow a systemic, procedural approach to discipline on the campus.
- Separate combinations of students who are extremely problematic when they are together (e.g., don't assign a critical mass of difficult students to one teacher if there is any way to avoid it).

Part of the role of the teacher is to understand that:

- The administrator is the backup system when all other approaches have failed.
- The teacher's system of discipline needs to be understood by the administrator in order to be supported.

4. Relationships of mutual respect with parents (there doesn't have to be agreement, but there does need to be respect)

In the chapter on parents (Stragegy 7), several tools are given to help work with them. These include a chart on subgroups of parents, ideas for parent involvement, and understanding overly protective parents.

5. Classroom and campus procedures

Ninety-five percent of discipline problems occur the first and last five minutes of class or during a transition. These tend to occur because there are not clear procedures.

What follows is a list of procedures that every teacher should have in place before school starts. To do so is to eliminate many problems.

Procedures Checklist

The following checklist is adapted from Guidelines for the First Days of School, from the Research Development Center for Teacher Education, Research on Classrooms, University of Texas, Austin.

Starting class	My procedure
• Taking attendance	
• Marking absences	
• Tardy students	
• Giving makeup work for absentees	
• Enrolling new students	
• Un-enrolling students	
• Students who have to leave school early	
• Warm-up activity (that students begin as soon as they walk into classroom)	

Other	My procedure
• Lining up for lunch/recess/special events	
• Walking to lunch/recess	
• Putting away coats and backpacks	
• Cleaning out locker	
• Preparing for fire drills and/or bomb threats	
• Going to gym for assemblies/pep rallies	
• Respecting teacher's desk and storage areas	
• Appropriately handling/using computers/ equipment	

Student accountability	My procedure
• Late work	
• Missing work	
• Extra credit	
• Redoing work and/or retaking tests	
• Incomplete work	
• Neatness	
• Papers with no names	

(continued on next page)

(continued from previous page)

Student accountability	My procedure
▪ Using pens, pencils, colored markers	
▪ Using computer-generated products	
▪ Internet access on computers	
▪ Setting and assigning due dates	
▪ Writing on back of paper	
▪ Makeup work and amount of time for makeup work	
▪ Use of mobile devices, headphones during class	
▪ Letting students know assignments missed during absence	
▪ Percentage of grade for major tests, homework, etc.	
▪ Explaining your grading policy	
▪ Letting new students know your procedures	
▪ Having contact with all students at least once during week	
▪ Exchanging papers	
▪ Using Internet for posting assignments and sending them in	

How will you ...	My plan
▪ Determine grades on report cards (components and weights of those components)?	
▪ Grade daily assignments?	
▪ Record grades so that assignments and dates are included?	
▪ Have students keep records of their own grades?	
▪ Make sure your assignments and grading reflect progress against standards?	
▪ Notify parents when students are not passing or having other academic problems?	

(continued on next page)

(continued from previous page)

How will you ...	My plan
▪ Contact parents if problem arises regarding student behavior?	
▪ Contact parents with positive feedback about their child?	
▪ Keep records and documentation of student behavior?	
▪ Document adherence to IEP (individualized education plan)?	
▪ Return graded papers in timely manner?	
▪ Monitor students who have serious health issues (peanut allergies, diabetes, epilepsy, etc.)?	

6. Mediation and consequences

Mediation means that the student understands the what, the why, and the how of the situation. Often when students are disciplined at school, they are told what they did and the consequences. Unless they're also instructed on why it's important to do (or not do) a certain behavior—and how to approach the situation the next time—there will be little change in student behavior.

7. Adult voice and reframing (so that the 80% of the discipline referrals that come from 11% of the staff can be addressed)

The concept of "voices" was coined by Eric Berne. He said there are three voices:

- A child (in conflict) who is whining
- A parent (in conflict) who is telling
- An adult (in conflict) who is asking questions for understanding

There are two kinds of parent voices—a positive and a negative. The positive is being firm and insistent, but the negative (in tone of voice and often with negative gestures, e.g., finger pointing, hands on hips, etc.) is when a "should" or "ought" message is being given. Claude Steiner, who worked with Berne, indicated that if you were forced to become your own parent quite young (or your primary caregiver was unsympathetic), then the tendency is to develop only two voices: the child voice and the negative parent voice.

A technique called reframing is used with the adult voice and can be very effective with both students and adults. It doesn't work if there's an addiction or biochemical issue. It also won't work if the issue isn't reframed to be compatible with the person's identity; as a general rule, people won't do anything that isn't compatible with their identity.

An example of reframing: When students physically fight, they often do so because it's seen as a sign of strength. When you tell students not to fight, they often interpret that to mean you want them to be wimps. They cannot live with that. But if you say, "Staying out of a fight takes more strength then getting in a fight," then the issue has been reframed. (Many students will tell you that isn't true, so I ask them if Michael Jordan the basketball player was tough, and they say yes, and then I have a Michael Jordan story I tell them.)

8. **Strategies for the 10% of students who cause 90% of the problems**

On most campuses around 10% of the students (sometimes a few more, sometimes a few less) create about 90% of the discipline problems. Often for these students there is a relationship issue. If you find a staff member who is genuinely interested in the student, have that staff member touch base with the student at least once a day and build a relationship of mutual respect with the student. Second, the student needs a positive group to belong to or a positive cause to support.

9. **An understanding of the law of truly large numbers**

What is the law of truly large numbers? It is a mathematical construct that basically states that when numbers become large, then the predictability and the patterns change. I have always considered it amazing that a high school of 3,000 students can be kept in line by 150–200 staff members or that a classroom of 30 students can be controlled by one person.

According to an article by Diaconis and Mosteller, with a large enough sample, any outrageous thing is likely to happen on any given day. J. E. Littlewood termed an event that occurs one in a million times to be "surprising." Taking this definition, more than 100,000 surprising events are "expected" each year in the United States alone and, in the world at large, Diaconis and Mosteller write that "we can be absolutely sure that we will see incredibly remarkable events."

A True Story

I know of a high school principal of a campus of about 3,000 students who decided that the most important part of his job at the beginning of the year was the enforcement of the dress code. So he instructed his teachers that the first 15 minutes of every day were to be spent on assessing dress code—and that any student not in compliance got sent to the office. Approximately 1,500 students got sent to the office the first day. It took office personnel all morning to write up the students and send them home. This happened every day for a month, at which point the principal decided the code could no longer be enforced. So the dress code was dropped. In the students' minds, they had won. Not surprisingly, overall behavior soon became a huge problem. Eventually, two to three days a week students would call in bomb threats and then be sent outside for a couple of hours. Students jumped over the fence and left. The school was out of control.

Contrast this story with another high school principal I know of who doesn't have big assemblies. Each year he goes to each English class and spends one class period talking to the students about his expectations for them and invites questions. He also invites them to talk to him when they need to do so. He establishes a relationship of respect with them but is very clear about the expectations and consequences. This school functions well.

THREE VOICES

Source: Adapted from
work of Eric Berne

The Child Voice *

Defensive, victimized, emotional, whining, losing
attitude, strongly negative non-verbal.

- Quit picking on me.
- You don't love me.
- You want me to leave.
- Nobody likes (loves) me.
- I hate you.
- You're ugly.

- You make me sick.
- It's your fault.
- Don't blame me.
- She, he, _____ did it.
- You make me mad.
- You made me do it.

* *The child voice is also playful, spontaneous, curious, etc. The phrases listed often occur in conflictual or manipulative situations and impede resolution.*

The Parent Voice * **

Authoritative, directive, judgmental, evaluative, win-lose mentality,
demanding, punitive, sometimes threatening.

- You shouldn't (should) do that.
- It's wrong (right) to do _____ .
- That's stupid, immature, out of line, ridiculous.
- Life's not fair. Get busy.
- You are good, bad, worthless, beautiful (any judgmental, evaluative comment).
- You do as I say.
- If you weren't so _____ , this wouldn't happen to you.
- Why can't you be like _____ ?

* *The parent voice can also be very loving and supportive. The phrases listed usually occur during conflict and impede resolution.*

** *The internal parent voice can create shame and guilt.*

The Adult Voice
Non-judgmental, free of negative non-verbal, factual,
often in question format, attitude of win-win.

- In what ways could this be resolved?
- What factors will be used to determine the effectiveness, quality of _____ ?
- I would like to recommend _____ .
- What are choices in this situation?
- I am comfortable (uncomfortable) with _____ .
- Options that could be considered are _____ .
- For me to be comfortable, I need the following things to occur _____ .
- These are the consequences of that choice/action _____ .
- We agree to disagree.

What Can You Do to Help Build Emotional Resources in Your Students?

"Feelings ... It seemed as if it were OK to step on your feelings and grind them down like snubbing out a worthless cigarette butt. It was as if you weren't 'worth' being nice to or cared for. Teachers, church people, and other respectable adults could talk in front of you about your family as if you couldn't hear, or it didn't matter. It's hard to grow a healthy self-concept when this is a common, everyday occurrence.

"I remember one Christmas in our little town where the annual Christmas parade was one of the biggest events of the year. My elementary school's float was a 'Choir of Angels.' I had been selected to be the featured angel at the front of the float. I was sitting there waiting for the parade to start feeling as pretty as a hood ornament on a Cadillac coupe. A couple of teachers walked by and one said, 'Oh, my God! How did this happen? She can't be the star of the float; everyone knows her father is the town drunk! Quick, move her to the back, and put a student up here whose parents are important!' I cried all the along the parade route. When I got home, my parents said they thought

I had told them I would be at the front of the float. I just couldn't tell them what had been said, so I started crying. I got a beating for lying ... again.

"In high school, I went up to my Geometry teacher and said, 'I don't understand how to do these problems. Would you help me?' She didn't even look at me or my paper, but said, 'Don't worry about it. You're getting them right.' However, what I heard her say was, 'Don't bother me. You don't matter enough for me to give you the time.' A classmate, whose father was president of the local bank, came up and asked the same question; she smiled and gave him help.

"That's why I was so happy to graduate from high school and have the opportunity to go off to college where no one would know about me or my family; I could start over and reinvent myself."

–Sue Nelle DeHart, Career Educator and aha! Process Consultant

Questions Students Can Use to Assess Their Own Emotional Resources

Resource: Emotional	Put a check here if this is true for you
▪ I often can't name the feelings I am having.	
▪ I often blame others for my feelings.	
▪ I lose my temper and yell at others.	
▪ I threaten and hit others and start fights.	
▪ When I am discouraged, I use drugs or alcohol to help me feel better.	
▪ I try to control the thoughts, feelings, and actions of others.	
▪ I have rigid rules for how others should act.	
▪ I often do things that I am sorry for later.	
▪ I act without thinking.	
▪ I sometimes harm myself physically.	
▪ I often have a negative attitude.	
▪ I sometimes use positive self-talk to help deal with problems.	
▪ I seldom lose my temper and yell at others.	

(continued on next page)

(continued from previous page)

Resource: Emotional	Put a check here if this is true for you
▪ I seldom get in fights or threaten others.	
▪ Sometimes I have positive thoughts and sometimes negative thoughts about the same person or situation.	
▪ I get along with others at school more often than not.	
▪ I have words for my feelings.	
▪ I use my thoughts to control my feelings.	
▪ I usually choose positive behaviors, even when I have strong negative feelings.	
▪ I can solve most problems with others by talking things through.	
▪ I mostly take responsibility for my own actions.	
▪ I identify my choices before I act.	
▪ I can set aside emotional issues and finish what I need to do at the time.	
▪ I make most of my decisions based upon future results rather than on how I feel at the time.	
▪ I help others see the positive in most situations.	
▪ I teach others about feelings and how to deal with them.	
▪ I can get along with many different people—different races, religions, political points of view, cultures, etc.	
▪ I look for ways to be stronger emotionally.	
▪ I can work through strong feelings without drugs and alcohol.	

Strategies to Encourage Appropriate Responses

Once the students have assessed their own emotional resources, interventions can include:

1. Give the words and phrases to address the feelings. For example, through pictures with young children and movie clips with older students, focus on expressions and gestures in the pictures and clips to assign vocabulary. Another example: What word would you use to say how he is feeling? What about her? Have you ever felt that way?

2. Teach positive self-talk through affirmations. Often students will initially reject positive self-talk. So then you approach it with "If … then …" statements. For example, if you can get a driver's license,

then you can pass this test. The brain will buy into the first part of the statement, and then the second part of the statement is believable because the first part is true. Many schools teach affirmations through journaling. For example, the teacher writes on the board, "Every day, in every way, I am becoming better and better." And then the student finds one example where this is true. (It may not be the example you want, but it's the beginning of positive thought.) Another one is "I am somebody, and I have something important to give to the world."

3. Give coping strategies. For example, ask questions to identify how the person could solve the problem, along with the choices that are available.

4. Provide stories of individuals who went through very difficult times and went on to become highly successful.

5. Have students develop a future story. You ask the students (in their mind) to make a movie of themselves in which they are the star. It would be a best-case-scenario movie—the best life possible. Then have them write that story and make a plan about how to get that life.

6. Be honest about the student's situation but don't show pity. I have said to students, "I respect so much what you deal with every day. I'm not sure I could deal with it. I can't change it for you. But I can give you the skills and tools you need so that you don't need to live that way all of your life, if you so desire."

Biochemical Issues

Sometimes no matter what the intervention is, it simply doesn't work. You may be dealing with a biochemical issue.

What are some indicators it may be a biochemical issue?

1. The behavior occurs without warning and often without provocation.

2. The behavior isn't predictable; there's no pattern.

3. The behavior has no advantage for the student. In other words, there isn't a payoff for the behavior. The student doesn't gain anything by engaging in the behavior.

4. The behavior often alienates other students.

5. The behavior doesn't respond to any cognitive interventions (behaviors controlled by one's thinking).

Biochemical issues are physical illnesses that affect thinking, emotions, and behavior. An analogy would be to diabetes. A person is a diabetic because the pancreas does not produce insulin. By providing insulin from an external source, the person can live a productive life. So it is with biochemical issues. When individuals can ingest the needed chemicals from an external source, they can be very productive.

At least five behavior disorders are considered to be biochemical. These are:

- Schizophrenia

- Obsessive-compulsive disorder (OCD)

- Attention deficit hyperactivity disorder (ADHD)

- Depression

- Bipolar disorder

The "bible" followed in the mental health field to diagnose disorders is the *Diagnostic and Statistical Manual of Mental Disorders* (DSM–5), Fifth Edition. It is published by the American Psychiatric Association and is available in or through most bookstores. This manual is highly technical. A companion book, *Clinician's Thesaurus: The Guide to Conducting Interviews and Writing Psychological Reports,* Sixth Edition (2005), by Edward L. Zuckerman is much more helpful due to its "translation" to more understandable language. The *Clinician's Thesaurus* contains many useful questions and criteria for discussion. Of particular benefit in the thesaurus are the extensive bibliography and research references.

A Summary of Key Factors Regarding Each of the Biochemical Issues

PLEASE NOTE: An accurate diagnosis can be made only by a trained developmental pediatrician, a psychiatrist, or a certified individual in the area of mental health. The purpose of this summary is simply to alert educators to the identifiers that may signal the need for referral to a trained professional.

It also should be noted that almost every human being likely will display some of these characteristics from time to time. The issue to note in biochemical issues is the number, frequency, and pervasiveness of the disorder. What is the pattern? In other words, can this student deal with reality in a constructive manner? Can the student relate to other people in a fairly consistent way with *mutual* respect and satisfaction?

For example, everyone from time to time is distracted, is angry, is impulsive, cannot sleep, etc. Does it occur once a month, every week, or every day? Does it disrupt the ability to have friends, succeed in school or at work, and/or cause damaging behaviors to self or others? It is the *pattern and the disruption* that begin to indicate the biochemical issue.

What is normal? The definitions are numerous. Sigmund Freud's definition was "to be able to work and love." Some define it as an absence of symptoms, nothing in excess, the mean. Others define it as the ability to have self-control, to be predictable, to use past experience, to be your own person (yet interact with others), and to be able to adapt to change.

In general, *the internal reality of an individual is usually shared by others in the external reality.* In other words, if you are the only person among many who is seeing snow, chances are that it is not snowing. No other person around you is experiencing that reality. What is normal is usually defined in relationship to a group of common behaviors, perceptions, and emotions, along with their lack of disruption in daily life.

Schizophrenia

The schizophrenic individual gives a common perception special or unusual significance, then elaborates or takes the perception into hallucination or delusion. Often voices are heard. The voices refer to the individual in the third person; the voices may make a monologue about the individual's behaviors/ thinking/feelings. One college sophomore who was schizophrenic didn't sleep all weekend and kept a Coke bottle by her bed. She believed that the 90-year-old man who was in the apartment above hers was going to come in at night and rape her. There was no evidence that he even knew that she lived in that apartment. The Coke bottle was going to be her main weapon of defense.

Obsessive-Compulsive Disorder (OCD)

The OCD individual engages in rituals for all manner of daily tasks and activities, including eating, sleeping, dressing, personal hygiene, school, and work. The individual may be compelled to engage in repetitions of a behavior— e.g., checking the locks repeatedly or washing hands constantly. The individual repeatedly touches, rubs, counts, and/or orders objects. In addition, sequences are very important. Hoarding and collecting can be indicators. One high school girl who is obsessive-compulsive writes down every word of the conversations she has had during the day as soon as she gets home. She does it every day. It is a ritual. It is a compulsion. She is obsessed by it. She dropped extracurricular activities so that she could reconstruct the conversations.

Attention Deficit Hyperactivity Disorder (ADHD)

The ADHD individual is in constant motion, is impulsive, often lacks fine-motor skills, is disorganized, has difficulty finishing tasks, does not focus, asks for repetitions of instruction, "doesn't listen," misses significant details, needs one-on-one supervision, is often unprepared. In general, the characteristics center around omissions, impulsivity, distractibility, attention variability, and physical motion.

Because the diagnosis of ADHD is fairly recent, many adults have ADHD and are not aware of it. In adults, it often surfaces in terms of impulsivity, poor time management, decisions that don't involve planning, poor emotional control, and inability to deal with long-term projects.

Depression

The depressed individual may have persistent physical symptoms that don't respond to treatment (headaches, pain, stomach issues). There's a negative view of much of life; decreased energy; substance abuse; distorted thinking; and a recent change in patterns of eating, sleeping, and relating to friends, work, and/or school.

Distorted thinking patterns may include the following: polarized (all or nothing), "binary" thinking; exaggerating or minimizing an event; drawing a negative conclusion when there's no support for one; attributing the cause of negative events to oneself; discounting any positive aspects; catastrophizing (going to the worst-case scenario); assigning feeling to thought ("because I'm angry he must be bad"); and referencing everything to something personal.

Bipolar Disorder (Often Referred to as Manic-Depressive Disorder)

The bipolar individual has extreme mood swings—from being overly gregarious, high-energy, going without sleep, cheerful, happy, and very active sexually to the very opposite. During the manic phase the individual may be self-important, controlling, challenging, vivacious, charming, and denying all criticism. But when individuals go to the other "pole," they become angry, insulting, uncooperative, critical, and abusive; severs relationships; blames; becomes silent, withdrawn, or depressed; and sleeps for long periods of time. What triggers the shift is not predictable. The shift can occur very quickly, without warning.

Non-Biochemical Issues

Things that affect school discipline tend to be a combination of environmental factors, external experiences, socioeconomic realities, racial and cultural issues, parental beliefs, etc. Of importance for educators are some pieces of information from the field of mental health.

Violence is correlated to the following factors: little or no impulse control; inability to plan; use of violence previously (against animals/objects or weaker, smaller people); taking pride in aggression; childhood exposure to violence, abuse, neglect, and/or instability (frequent changes of residence); substance abuse; and availability of weapons or victims.

Zuckerman refers to the developmental stages of conduct disorder: "Difficult temperament, hyperactivity, overt conduct problems and aggressiveness, poor social relationships, academic problems, truancy/stealing/substance use, association with deviant peers, delinquency/arrest, recidivism." According to Zuckerman, "[P]rognosis is worsened by ADHD, parental rejection, harsh discipline, absence of a father, delinquent friends, [and] parental substance abuse."

Are There Now More Biochemical Issues, or Are We Simply Better at Identifying Them?

The answer to both of these questions is yes. The research is that there are more chemicals in food, in the environment, in the water, etc. Biochemical issues also can be inherited. And because of the work that has been done in this area, more identification also is occurring.

How Do We Begin to Address a Biochemical Issue?

The place to begin is almost always a series of cognitive interventions to change behaviors. When those fail, the next step is to refer the issue to a professional: a developmental pediatrician, a psychiatrist, a mental health professional, et al. Most principals and teachers are not qualified to diagnose.

Often among educators there is a belief that, through determination and effort, behaviors can change. For many behaviors, that is correct. If the behavior has a biochemical basis, however, the student may need additional professional and/or medical assistance to make the transition to a different set of behaviors. As the research sheds more light on these topics, our ability to create safer schools will increase.

Physical safety usually has an overlay of emotional safety. If a student hasn't had the opportunity to have nurturing, safe relationships outside of school, then it will be difficult for that student to have them in school, unless specific understandings, instructions, and disciplines are present.

Steps to Follow

1. Have a campuswide plan that identifies appropriate behaviors and responses.

2. Direct-teach those behaviors and responses.

3. Build relationships of mutual respect with students.

4. On large campuses, work with classrooms rather than large assemblies to teach and address student needs.

5. Identify the 10% of students creating the majority of discipline issues and determine the best interventions for those students. Are there relationship issues? Are there issues of not knowing appropriate responses? Are there biochemical issues?

6. Have a process in place for addressing biochemical issues.

7. Require that each teacher identify in writing the procedures that will be used in the classroom; use the procedures checklist from earlier in this chapter.

8. Teach the adult voice to staff. Address the 11% of the staff who are responsible for 80% of the referrals, which almost always happen because the adult is in the negative parent voice.

Strategy 6

Use a Six-Step Process to Keep Track of Every Student's Learning

*"I have, over 46 years in the education profession, come to realize that people, regardless of their age, are doing as well as they can do given what they know at the moment. So if you can begin to change not only what they know, but how they **know** they know, or how they learn, then you're going to see a big difference. Before we started the aha! Process model we had a great achievement gap between students who come from affluent homes and students and children who come from homes in poverty. What's happened in our district is really interesting. All achievement scores have gone up—but at the same time. Students who come from homes of poverty are closing that achievement gap. So not only are they catching up with their peers, as our test scores go up exponentially, they are right there with them. We were one of the schools recognized by Standard & Poor's for closing the achievement gaps among all of our subpopulations. That's what made a difference for us."*

—Dr. Wynona Winn, Superintendent of Schools

As schools are required to address accountability, it becomes necessary to keep track of the learning of each individual student. In the history of schooling in the United States, we first kept track of attendance by individual student. Then we gave grades by individual student, after which we kept records of the courses and credits by individual student. Now we're asked to keep track of learning against standards by individual student. To do that, there must be a system in place.

Issues in Student Achievement and School Accountability

1. Achievement is based on test scores.

2. Accountability (adequate yearly progress) is a numbers construct representing equity and excellence.

3. Because many students come from a situated-learning environment and because survival in school is decontextualized learning, transfer requires extra supports in instruction, i.e., mental models.

Research Findings

Eliyahu Goldratt states the following in his book *Theory of Constraints*: "The three distinct states that every science has gone through are: classification, correlation, and *effect-cause-effect*."

For example, the Greeks classified the stars and called it astrology. Ptolemy in Alexandria stated that planets move along a circle—the first correlation. Copernicus stated that the sun was the center of the circle. Kepler postulated that the planets were not on a circle but elliptical in their movement—all correlations. This became astronomy. Newton then asked the question *Why??* He suggested that if any two bodies attract each other in proportion to their masses and in reciprocal proportion to the distance between them, then we can explain effects in nature (the gravitational law). Continues Goldratt:

> The widely accepted approach is to define science as the search for a minimum number of assumptions that will enable us to explain, by direct logical deduction, the maximum number of natural phenomena … Science does not concern itself with truths but with validity (pages 22–27).

In the business of education, we have gone through classification of students and schools, e.g., Special Education students, Limited English Language students, et al. The research on teaching and instruction has been correlational.

Now we are moving to *effect-cause-effect*, which answers the question why. This chapter is about moving to the effect-cause-effect method of tracking student learning. Goldratt goes on to say:

> What is not well appreciated is that the effect-cause-effect stage brings with it some significant ramifications that we have to adjust to. It involves a different approach to untying a subject. It also gives us the ability to change the system in which we operate, but in doing so it obsoletes for a while our intuition on how to operate in this new environment (pages 28–29).

Research Findings with Our School Improvement Process

In Appendix E you will find the research that we at aha! Process have done with this school-improvement process. The research from several sites indicates that the implementation of this process has statistically significant results at the .001 level.

> *"I think they [the quarterly benchmarks] help you focus on the content, what you're trying to teach kids, what you want kids to learn. I think when it comes to the curriculum, there is a hidden curriculum, and there is a taught curriculum, and [the benchmarks] help you focus on the taught curriculum. The benchmarks are important because they help you monitor the progress of students. At the same time, [the benchmarks] kind of impress upon teachers that you're not trying to hide information from students. When you test them, you're not trying to trick them, you're trying to show them what you expect them to learn. If they can answer those questions, then they have met your expectations in terms of learning.*

> *"Quartiling ... that was interesting and that was new. It gave us a reason to focus on data; people are always talking about data. This data and that data—and you don't know what to do with it. When Ruby came along and started talking about quartiling (take your state scores, for example; you put your students in four different quartiles and move those students throughout the quartiles as they go about their education) it gives you something visible to focus on. You can visually see the improvement in students as they move from one quartile to another quartile. So I would say it gives teachers an opportunity to focus on progress, on test scores, and it gives them a vehicle to use as they go about that process."*

> –Dr. Neal Brown, High School Principal

A Six-Step Process to Keep Track of All Students and Their Learning
Against Accountability Measures (for examples of each of these, see Appendix B for secondary schools and Appendix C for elementary schools)

Schools have processes for accounting (requisitions, purchase orders, etc.). There also must be a systematic process for keeping track of student learning.

Benjamin Bloom did extensive research to determine what makes a difference in learning. He identified four factors:

- The amount of time to learn
- The intervention(s) of the teacher
- How clear the focus of the instruction is
- What the student came in knowing

The control the individual teacher has over these variables is significantly impacted by what is happening on the campus. When interventions are addressed at a campus level in a systematic way, more learning occurs.

The first process is to know where individual students are performing against the larger accountability frame.

Key Question: How are our individual students performing against a larger population?

Process 1: Gridding Individual Student Performance

Gridding student achievement against the subgroups for AYP and the categories of state assessment or quartiles is critical for determining where the current performance is. (Only one test per content per grade level or course is used.)

Many schools look at the patterns of the larger group, i.e., how the students are doing against a particular objective. While that is important, the most essential part of this process is to look at the individual students *first*. **Accountability is based on numbers of students in a given category and the number or percentage of students who are moving to another category. It is not based on the group average.**

Therefore, the first step is to grid the students at each grade level or course by making this chart.

Test Band	Caucasian	African American	Hispanic	Native American	Asian	Second Language	Special Education	Title I
75–100%								
50–74%	Johnny							Johnny
25–49%								
0–24%								
Students who were exempt								

Most states have four categories of performance, along these lines: Exemplary, Recognized, Acceptable, Needs Improvement. Each state has its own terminology. If there isn't a state assessment, then use the quartile breakdowns.

Steps for Completing the Chart

1. Have each teacher identify *by student name* the level of performance. For example, Johnny may have been in the second quartile in reading, and he is Caucasian, so his name goes in that box. He also may be on free and reduced-price lunch, so his name goes in that box too. All students are recorded. If there are no test data for the student, the teacher gives a "mock" assessment and based on those data, the teacher makes a determination about the approximate performance level of the student. One table is done for reading, one for math, one for writing, and one for any other subject area for which the school is held accountable. At the secondary level, it may be done by course.

2. The principal or counselor identifies the *number* of students at a grade level or in a course.

3. The principal has each teacher count the number of students in the top two categories and give the principal the number. The principal gets from all the teachers the number of students at a grade level in a subject area/course who are in the top two quartiles.

4. The principal calculates the percentage of students who are in the top two quartiles. For example, if there are 100 students in that grade level or course and 80 out of a 100 students are in the top two quartiles, then it has a percentage of 80%. (It has been my personal observation— based on experience in many states and districts—that a campus needs to have 80% of its students in the top two categories to have "respectable" performance on state accountability instruments.)

5. Then the dialogue begins. What students do we have who can move up a category? Why is this student in this category? What interventions do we need to use? Does this student have relationships of mutual respect in this building? Which students are counted twice?

KEY QUESTION: What do students actually get the opportunity to learn, and how much time do they get to learn it?

Process 2: Establishing a Relationship Between Content and Time

Reasonable expectations (time and content grids). This is a simpler model of curriculum mapping that addresses the focus of instruction and the amount of time. Reasonable expectations identify what is taught and the amount of time devoted to it. This allows a campus to "data mine," i.e., determine the payoff between what actually gets taught, the amount of time given to it and the corresponding test results. For example, if two hours a day are spent on reading, but only 15 minutes is devoted to students actually reading, the payoff will be less than if 45 minutes of that time is devoted to students actually reading.

The big misuse of these reasonable expectations (often called pacing guides) is that they aren't used for professional dialogue. If they're developed by the district and don't include professional dialogue, they don't work well.

The purpose of this tool is to facilitate a dialogue about instruction, curriculum, and pedagogy.

Simple Yet Effective Tools and Processes

One of the first pieces of information that a principal and campus need to know is what is actually being taught. Here's a simple process to help find this out.

1. If you are on a six-week grading period, divide a paper into six equal pieces. If you are on a nine-weeks grading period, divide a paper into four equal pieces. Have each teacher for each subject area write the units or skills they teach in each grading period. In other words, what do they usually manage to teach to that grade level in that subject area in that amount of time?

(continued on next page)

(continued from previous page)

2. Have each grade level meet and discuss one subject area at a time. Have teachers bring three things: the paper from Step One, the state-mandated standards, and the test scores. Then you say, "Here is what you taught and spent time on, here is what you were supposed to teach, and here is what you got. Based on these three things, what should we focus on to raise achievement?" Then through professional dialogue, the teachers come to a consensus on the expectations for that grade level.

3. Have the faculty as a group compare grade levels 1 through 5 or 6 through 8 or 9 through 12. If Johnny was with the school for five years, what would he have the opportunity to learn? What would he not have had the opportunity to learn? Where are the holes in the opportunities to learn?

4. The faculty then uses this information to identify the strengths and weaknesses in the current educational program. Are some things repeated without benefit to achievement? Are some things not ever taught or so lightly brushed to not be of benefit? What is included that could be traded out for something that has a higher payoff in achievement?

5. When the discussion is over, the one-page sheets are revised and given to the appropriate teachers.

6. Twice a year the principal meets with grade-level teams and, using these sheets, discusses the progress of the learning, the adjustments that need to be made, etc. These become working documents. Because of their simplicity, they can be easily revised.

What follows are the steps used to develop time and content grids. This should be revisited at the beginning of the year and again at mid-year by the grade level and the principal—or the course teachers and the department chair. The chart below describes the process used.

How often do you use the time and content grids?

"Every day, all the time. We use our time and content grids as roadmaps for our grade level. Without them our grade level would be lost on how to collaborate with one another effectively. The time and content grids started with just Language Arts and Math. Since then, we found them to be so valuable that we now have them in every subject area, which allow us as a grade level to successfully plan and use thematic instruction. It also encourages us to collaborate daily, even when we have very little planning time.

> *"My other half of the day is spent as an ESL (English as a Second Language) teacher where it is a pullout program. The time and content grids with each grade level let me to know exactly what the general education teacher is working on, even when we are not able to meet face to face. They enable me to link my instruction in the ESL classroom to the general education classroom and bridge that gap in between the two. The time and content grids help us work together to create identical benchmark tests and activities that go along with our state-mandated standards. The time and content grid has probably been the best tool we have received from Ruby. This tool helps us grow professionally and helps us better instruct the students so they can grow academically. We know that sometimes we have to stray from the time and content grids because of the analyzed data and student needs, but they are definitely helpful roadmaps for us to follow."*

> —Susanne Tieman, Third-Grade Teacher and ESL Teacher

KEY QUESTION: What was the quality of teaching?

Process 3: High-Quality Instruction—Teaching

What is high-quality teaching? Much research has been done on the subject. High-quality teaching includes classroom management, instruction, and content understanding and knowledge.

High-quality teaching also involves the nature of the assignments. In the research this is called curriculum calibration.

The following is from a research study by John Hollingsworth and Silvia Ybarra called "Analyzing Classroom Instruction: Curriculum Calibration."

Grade	Mathematics GLS * % * grade-level standards						Average Grade Level	Language Arts GLS %						Average Grade Level
	K	1	2	3	4	5		K	1	2	3	4	5	
K	100							100						K
1st		100					1.0		100					1.0
2nd		23	77				1.8		20	80				1.8
3rd			45	55			2.6		2	14	84			2.8
4th			40	40	20		2.8		2	30	35	33		3.0
5th		2	35	59	2	2	2.7			28	60	10	2	2.9

Hollingsworth and Ybarra state:

> According to the [preceding] table, kindergarten and first grade are being taught at grade level. Curriculum slippage begins at second grade where only 77% of the math material and 80% of the language arts material being presented to the students is on grade level. By the fifth grade, only 2% of the work being given to the students is on grade level. Keep in mind that we calibrated every assignment that the students were being asked to do. By the fifth grade, the student assignments were mostly second- and third-grade material. An ironic note is that these below-grade-level assignments were full of happy faces, "good work," "A+," etc. These students knew the material and needed to have the level of instruction ratcheted up. Instruction at this school was miscalibrated.

Categories of Instructional Strategies That Affect Student Achievement				
Category	**Ave. Effect Size (ES)**	**Percentile Gain**	**No. of ESs**	**Standard Deviation (SD)**
Identifying similarities and differences	1.61	45	31	.31
Summarizing and note taking	1.00	34	179	.50
Reinforcing effort and providing recognition	.80	29	21	.35
Homework and practice	.77	28	134	.36
Nonlinguistic representations	.75	27	246	.40
Cooperative learning	.73	27	122	.40
Setting objectives and providing feedback	.61	23	408	.28
Generating and testing hypothesis	.61	23	63	.79
Questions, cues, and advance organizers	.59	22	1251	.26

Note: We caution readers that it is impossible to derive the average effect sizes shown in this figure from the effect-size information provided in the figures Chapters 2–10 [in Marzano's book], which list the synthesis studies used in the analysis of the instructional strategy under discussion. The synthesis studies listed for a given category of instructional strategy often involve the review of some of the same research, and thus involve some of the same comparisons between experimental and control groups. An "average of these averages" would lead to inaccurate conclusions. The average effect sizes reported in Figure 1.3 are based on comparisons that are independent. Since these averages do not include overlapping data, they provide a more accurate summary statement about the effect of a particular category of instructional strategy.

Source: *Classroom Instruction That Works: Research-Based Strategies for Increasing Student Achievement* by Robert J. Marzano, Debra J. Pickering, and Jane E. Pollock.

Additional research by Marzano, Pickering, and Pollock identifies these strategies having a high correlation to student achievement.

KEY QUESTION: How do you know they are learning?

Process 4: Measuring the Learning—Formative Assessments

There may have been wonderful teaching, but learning may not have occurred.

Grades Are Not a Measure of Growth Against Standards

Many educators want to use grades as the measurement of learning. But grades rarely measure against standards and are often a compilation of effort, compliance (i.e., handing in things), and group work.

What Are Formative Assessments?

Formative assessments are methods for identifying and assessing the growth a student makes on a regular basis.

How Do You Develop Formative Assessments?

Using roving substitutes to relieve teachers is one of the best ways to develop formative assessments. Teachers are out of the classroom for only a half-day—or two class periods at the high school. During this time teachers develop formative assessments for the next grading period.

Kinds of Formative Assessments

Several growth assessments are available. What makes something a growth assessment is that it identifies movement against a constant set of criteria. What makes a growth assessment different from a test is that the criteria do not change in a growth assessment.

Benchmarks

This is a simpler model of three or four indicators by grading period to show whether a student needs an immediate intervention. Critical markers are very simple. They identify the critical attributes that students must acquire each six weeks if they are to progress. If the student has not demonstrated these benchmarks, then immediate additional interventions must begin. How does one get benchmarks? Once again, identify the experienced educators who invariably have high student achievement. Ask them how they know a student will have trouble. They already know the criteria. And by putting it in writing and having a common understanding, teachers, particularly those who are new to teaching or who are not as experienced, can more readily make interventions and address student progress. It then needs to go back to the grade level for feedback and changes.

Rubrics

To develop a rubric, a simple process can be used.

Have the teachers in your building (who consistently get the highest achievement, as well as understand the district curriculum and standards) develop the growth assessment. Keep in mind these three guidelines:

1. The purpose is to identify the desired level of achievement.

2. The growth assessment needs to be simple and easily understood.

3. Student movement or growth toward the desired level of achievement needs to be clear.

Steps for creating rubrics:

1. Identify three to five criteria.

2. Set up a grid with numerical values (1 through 4 is usually enough).

3. Identify what would be an excellent piece of work or demonstration. That becomes number 4.

4. Work backwards. Next identify what would be a 3 and so on.

When the rubric is developed, it needs to go back to the faculty for feedback and refinement. When there is substantial agreement and at least 80% buy-in, the faculty moves forward with it.

Ten-Question Tests

Ten-question tests are questions that are added to a six-week test to "dipstick" for students' progress against the standards. There can be 20 questions or 25. We just chose 10 because it's easier to monitor. Teachers make up the questions or choose the questions they wish to use.

Steps for creating 10-question tests:

1. Bring together test questions already used.

2. Code test questions of the standards.

3. Use the time and content grids to identify the standards taught by grading period.

4. Sort/eliminate questions by standards; find questions that best assess that standard.

5. Embed these questions into each teacher's test for the grading period.

Mock State Assessments/End-of-Course Test

1. Put all students in that course or on that grade level in an altered schedule for one day to take the mock assessment.

2. Have the students score their own tests (exception is writing).

3. The students grid their performance against the standards.

4. A letter is sent to the parent(s) explaining the student's current status against the state assessment. The letter explains that this outcome is a possibility given that the mock test is not exactly the same test as the state test.

5. Assign to tutoring those students who are at risk.

Using Student Artifacts

To check curriculum calibration, student work is examined against rubrics and the standards.

KEY QUESTION: What do you do when they did not learn it?

Process 5: Interventions

When students are identified through the formative assessments as making inadequate growth, immediate interventions are provided for those students.

The issue here is that the intervention be timely and occur at a classroom and on a campus level. One other point is simply that for optimal learning, the student needs to stay with the regular instruction, inasmuch as possible, to have the opportunity to learn what the other students are learning. Additional time for learning must be found, e.g., using Social Studies time to teach Nonfiction Reading.

To begin sorting for the causes of inadequate growth, these questions are asked:

1. Is there a relationship issue? Does the student have a group to belong to?
2. Is there an issue with the paper world—the abstract representational world?
3. Is it a resource issue?
4. Is there a skills issue?
5. Is there a biochemical issue?
6. Is there a curriculum issue? (Was it actually taught?)
7. Did the student have enough time to learn it?
8. Was the work assigned on grade level (curriculum calibration)?

KEY QUESTION: What is the key motivator in student learning?

A relationship of mutual respect

KEY QUESTION: How do you make sure this process occurs on a systematic basis?

Process 6: Embedding These Processes into the Schedule So That Professional Time Is Devoted to It

For these processes to occur, they must be embedded into the daily life of the school, which includes:

1. Being on the school calendar before the school year starts
2. Getting substitutes for the roving-sub days when these items are developed
3. Identifying common planning time that can be used
4. Setting the days that the principal or department chair will meet with the team

Just as we have processes for accounting, purchasing, and the like, we must have processes for monitoring student learning.

Steps to Follow

1. Place each student on a grid by individual performance.

2. Know what is being taught and how much time is given to that particular content or skill.

3. Provide high-quality instruction.

4. Give formative assessments against the standards (grades typically don't tell growth against standards) to determine to what extent learning is occurring.

5. By individual student, determine interventions immediately if learning is not occurring (campuswide interventions must be available).

6. Use a professional, collegial process that is embedded into the campus plan so that it occurs routinely.

EDITOR'S NOTE: The preceding six processes have been expanded and refined and are outlined in *School Improvement: 9 Systemic Processes to Raise Achievement* by Ruby Payne and Donna Magee. For more information about the workbook and workshops, visit ahaprocess.com.

Strategy ⑦

Build Relationships of Mutual Respect with Parents

Use multiple methods for parent involvement; develop strategies for conferences with parents

"Showing mutual respect at Southwick is something that I have put as a top priority. And the aha! Process training certainly helped embed that even more; it gives me more reason to work at it on a daily basis with my parents.

"A great example is a mom we didn't think would come in for the intervention team. Here at a table sit the classroom teacher, the Special Ed teacher, the Literacy teacher, me ... and we're all around the table talking about this young man, this second-grade boy's issues, and he's had a lot of learning problems. And so we were trying to come up with some good ideas, and we never dreamed the mom would come because normally she just hasn't made good connections with us. We looked up and were so surprised to see her walk in the door.

"We said, 'Oh, we're so glad you're here,' and she said, 'Well, I know you're just going to do what you're going to do. There's no reason for me to come. So why should I even come? But I decided I would, but I know you're just going to do what you're going to do.'

"And one teacher sat down next to her and just took a moment to talk to her really sincerely, one on one, saying, 'You have to understand that at Southwick your voice is important, and we need your voice at this table because your son is important to us, and we know you love your son. So we want you to be a part of this.'

"By the time we got done an hour later, it was probably one of the best conferences we have ever had with a parent. I knew when she walked in the door that it took a lot of courage for her to come. She didn't like the setting, and it was kind of scary to walk in a room with all these teachers sitting around. But the one teacher who took the time to say, 'Your voice counts, and you're important' just made all the difference in the world.

"One hour later, we were laughing and talking about all the things we're going to try, and we were honoring all of her ideas because we found out that she had been doing far more with her son than any teacher there could imagine she was doing—and it was starting to pay off.

"So we won both ways. Both of us—the mother and the staff—walked away from that conference having more respect for one another because we took the time to listen and find out."

–Dr. Jeanne Zehr, Title I Area Administrator

How Do You Work with Parents?

Most new teachers report that their greatest difficulties are discipline and working with parents.

Why are parents important? Well, to state what may be obvious … parents first and foremost are the primary external support system for the child, and their beliefs and attitudes naturally have a significant impact on the thinking and actions of the child. Success in school in the United States requires that a student have a strong external support system because of homework, projects, money, time, etc., that the school needs. Parents also represent the community in which the student lives.

An important contributing factor to the success of a student in school is the extent to which the external support system exists.

A SYSTEM is where individuals have rules, roles, and relationships.

A DYSFUNCTIONAL SYSTEM is one in which individuals cannot get their basic needs met.

A SUPPORT SYSTEM is individuals and/or a group who promote, protect, and assist the student.

All systems are, to some extent, dysfunctional. A system is not equally functional or dysfunctional for each individual within a given system. The extent to which individuals must give up meeting most of their needs in order to meet the needs of other people is the extent to which the situation is dysfunctional.

Question:

Why would support systems have such importance in school and at work?

Answer:

Support systems provide resources and tools to students so they can devote time to learning and to personal development.

Whether there will be a support system for the student depends in part on whether there's a support system for the adult. Who supports the adult? If the adult has no support system, chances are good that the support system for the student will be thin or nonexistent.

What Do Multiple Systems of Support Look Like for Parents?

Building Communities of Support

The layering and structuring of "practices that contribute to student engagement and high school completion" constitute the basic concept in communities of support. "Chief among these is the ability of school personnel to create communities of support that are concerned about how students perform and express that concern in genuine, effective, caring ways" (The El Puente Project). So how does one do that? One way is to create a scaffolding of interventions. The other is by creating linkages to community groups.

The Following Suggestions Can Help Create Communities of Support for Parents:

1. **Mutual respect:** Parents are welcomed by first-line staff. Parents are welcome in the building. Accusatory and blaming language is not present.

2. **School design teams:** A cross-section of staff, parents, law enforcement, ministers, and students who identify issues of support.

3. **Home contacts:** These are not home visits but quick five-minute visits to the home at the beginning of the school year to say hello. Substitutes are used a couple of days so teachers can do this late afternoons and early evenings the first or second week of school.

4. **Videos:** These can be made by the staff and students to introduce faculty, to tell about school discipline programs, to highlight upcoming events, etc.

5. **Student and parent voices:** Through informal conversation (not meetings), parents and students are asked what the school could do to better serve them.

6. **Weekend activities:** Friday evenings, Saturday mornings, and Sunday afternoons work the best.

7. **Varied and targeted parental involvement activities:** Free donuts for dads the first Monday of every month. Carnations for moms. Lunch for grandparents. Picnics for people who live in the student's house.

8. **Support mechanisms for parents that involve follow-up:** 3x5 cards with the steps that will be followed. Magnets for the refrigerator that list school phone numbers and holidays. Stickers that parents can give to the child for good behaviors.

9. **Informal coffee klatches:** Counselor or principal asks a parent with whom there is already a relationship to invite three or four other friends over for coffee in the parent's home. The principal or counselor brings the donuts. This is a forum for an informal discussion about what bothers parents, what they would like to see, what they like, etc.

10. **Overcoming reluctance to participate by creating one-on-one relationships.**

11. **Tools for dealing with parent/teacher conferences.**

12. **Tools for dealing with difficult parents.**

13. **Simple written documents that have pictures and words and/or cartoons.**

14. **Using networking capabilities in the community:** Make a flier with cartoons that is one page and has an advertisement for a business in the community on the back. Introduce your faculty through cartoons. The advertiser pays for the paper and the printing. Distribute them to beauty salons, grocery stores, barbershops, churches, etc., much like a local community shopper or merchandiser.

15. **Information for parents that enhances their lives:** Offer information like how to fix bad credit (knowledge about money), how to manage a difficult boss (conflict-resolution skills), etc.

16. **Information on video or in cartoon that helps parents deal with their children, i.e., how to enhance obedience in your child.**

17. **Giving awards to parents:** A child identifies something a parent has done. On a Saturday morning the child gives a certificate to the parent and thanks the parent.

18. **Parent/teacher conferences led by the student.**

19. **Weekend activities that use the computers and athletic facilities of the campus.**

20. **Partnering with a school that has strong parent involvement.**

21. **Peer-mediation training for students:** They teach it to parents informally.

22. **Teaching students to be better friends:** Have students list the five friends they go to when they have a problem. Tally who are the "best friends." Teach them how to ask questions to solve problems. Teach them how to identify which problems are serious and need to be referred, such as deep depression or threats of suicide.

23. **Teaching parents to be better friends to other adults.**

24. **Block parties:** Get a street blocked off for an afternoon and have a party.

In other words, creating communities of support is a layered, varied set of interventions and activities. The idea that a school can have "x" number of meetings a year—a Halloween party and a spring carnival—isn't enough. What works best is a scaffolding of interventions.

What Does the Research Say?

What the Research Says About Parent Involvement in Children's Education in Relation to Academic Achievement

Where Children Spend Their Time

- School-age children spend 70% of their waking hours (including weekends and holidays) outside of school.

When Parents Get Involved

- The earlier in a child's educational process parent involvement begins, the more powerful the effects.
- The most effective forms of parent involvement are those that engage parents in working directly with their children on learning activities at home.

Impact

- Eighty-six percent of the general public believes that support from parents is the most important way to improve the schools.
- Lack of parental involvement is the biggest problem facing public schools.
- Decades of research show that when parents are involved students have:
  - Higher grades, test scores, and graduation rates
  - Better school attendance
  - Increased motivation, better self-esteem
  - Lower rates of suspension
  - Decreased use of drugs and alcohol
  - Fewer instances of violent behavior
- Family participation in education was twice as predictive of students' academic success as family socioeconomic status. Some of the more intensive programs had effects that were 10 times greater than other factors.
- The more intensely parents are involved, the more beneficial the achievement effects.
- The more parents participate in schooling in a sustained way at every level—in advocacy, decision making, and oversight roles, as fund-raisers and boosters, as volunteers and paraprofessionals, and as home teachers—the better for student achievement.

(continued on next page)

(continued from previous page)

Parent Expectations and Student Achievement

- The most consistent predictors of children's academic achievement and social adjustment are parent expectations of the child's academic attainment and satisfaction with their child's education at school.

- Parents of high-achieving students set higher standards for their children's educational activities than parents of low-achieving students.

Major Factors of Parent Involvement

- Three major factors of parent involvement in the education of their children:

  1. Parents' beliefs about what is important, necessary, and permissible for them to do with, and on behalf of, their children.

  2. The extent to which parents believe that they can have a positive influence on their children's education.

  3. Parents' perceptions that their children and school want them to be involved.

Types of Involvement

- Although most parents don't know how to help their children with their education, with guidance and support they may become increasingly involved in home learning activities and find themselves with opportunities to teach, to be models for, and to guide their children.

- When schools encourage children to practice reading at home with parents, the children make significant gains in reading achievement compared with those who practice only at school.

- Parents who read to their children, have books available, take trips, guide TV watching, and provide stimulating experiences contribute to student achievement.

- Families whose children are doing well in school usually exhibit the following characteristics:

  1. Establish a daily family routine. Examples: Providing time and a quiet place to study, assigning responsibility for household chores, being firm about bedtime, and having the evening meal together.

  2. Monitor out-of-school activities. Examples: Setting limits on screen time, checking up on children when parents are not home, and arranging for after-school activities and supervised care.

(continued on next page)

(continued from previous page)

3. Model the value of learning, self-discipline, and hard work. Examples: Communicating through questioning and conversation, demonstrating that achievement comes from working hard.

4. Express high but realistic expectations for achievement. Examples: Setting goals and standards that are appropriate for children's age and maturity, recognizing and encouraging special talents, informing friends and family about successes.

5. Encourage children's development/progress in school. Examples: Maintaining a warm and supportive home, showing interest in children's progress at school, helping with homework, discussing the value of a good education and possible career options, and staying in touch with teachers and school staff.

6. Encourage reading, writing, and discussions among family members. Examples: Reading, listening to children read, and talking about what is being read.

Student Interest

- Most students at all levels—elementary, middle, and high school—want their families to be more knowledgeable partners about schooling and are willing to take active roles in assisting communications between home and school.

- When parents come to school on a reasonably regular basis, it reinforces in the child's mind that school and home are connected and that school is an integral part of the family's life.

School and District Leadership

- The strongest and most consistent predictors of parent involvement at school and at home are the specific school programs and teacher practices that encourage that involvement at school, as well as guide parents in how to help their children at home.

- School-initiated activities to help parents change the home environment can have a strong influence on children's school performance.

- Parents need specific information on how to help and what to do.

Source: Adapted from Michigan Department of Education, "Collaborating for Success—Parent Engagement Toolkit."

What Are the Three Styles of Parenting and Discipline?

In the research on parenting, three styles of discipline are used (and/or a mix of the three):

Permissive, authoritarian, and negotiated

For an individual to be self-governing, three constructs must be understood: choice, consequence, and parameters. Parameters are those lines that cannot be crossed. For example, you cannot drink and drive. When a parent is permissive, the child understands choices but not consequences or parameters. When a parent is authoritarian, the child understands consequences and parameters but not choices. When there is a negotiated approach to discipline, then the child understands all three. Many parents use a mix. When the approach goes back and forth, from one to the other, it is very confusing for the child.

How Administrators Can Support Teachers When Parents Are Difficult

By setting up parameters and boundaries

For example: Is this something you want me to listen to or something you want me to do something about? If it's something you want me to do something about, then the teacher must be involved, e.g., have you talked to the teacher first?

By establishing a safety network for students

In other words, keeping track of every student. One of the ways we did it at the elementary school when I was a principal was to have a meeting once a month with a team of people: counselor, psychologist, nurse, learning support teacher, et al., and we hired a substitute who went from class to class for 15 minutes at a time. Teachers would sign up for 15-minute intervals to talk about students for whom interventions had not worked, and then we would set up an integrated plan to address the issue.

By establishing norms for school behavior

It is unacceptable to allow a parent to engage in behaviors that students are not allowed to engage in. One of the things a principal does is identify what is and is not acceptable. For example, if parents come in cussing, the parents are brought into the office and told privately that the next time the parents may cuss only in the privacy of the office—or they will be asked by the law to leave.

By establishing a climate of mutual respect for students *and* parents

When I was a principal, I found out that some of my teachers were hanging up on parents when they called. I stated that working with parents had to be a two-way street. If we wanted them to take us seriously when we called them, then we needed to do the same in return. So it was agreed that there would be no more hanging up on parents.

Another way parents are given mutual respect is how they are greeted when they call or come visit the school—the non-verbals in particular. One day I went to my son's high school to give him something, and the treatment I received was incredibly rude. The attitude seemed to be: *We don't want you here. You are not even worth my time.* I wondered how a parent who has no attachment to schooling would feel about such treatment.

By listening to parents

Almost all parents deeply love their children. Nothing can put a deeper fear into parents than to think that their child is being harmed in some way—and that they have no power over the situation. So it's important that you listen for what is not said. What is the fear? What is the underlying (often unspoken) need? Are there ways to address the situation so that the parents can be assured that their child is safe and cared for by the school?

By managing the people above you

Let your boss know about any issues—particularly sensitive issues or a difficult parent. Your boss can then support you when that individual goes to see your boss or when the rumors begin to fly. Always keep your boss informed.

Parent Involvement

Do not confuse having physical presence with parent involvement. The research seems to indicate that when a parent provides support, insistence, and expectations to the child, the presence or absence of a parent in the physical school building is immaterial. Therefore, training for parents should concentrate on these issues.

What Subgroups of Parents Do You Have?

Think of parents not as a single group but as distinct subgroups.

Niche marketing is a term used in advertising. Simply put, it means that one size does not fit all and that marketing needs to be targeted to specific audiences. The following table outlines some of the subgroups of parents found in many schools, along with ideas for involvement in their child's education. As noted above, a parent does not need to physically come to the school to be involved.

Put these activities into the site-based plan so that they occur. The activities actually become a marketing plan for the campus.

Subgroups of parents	Ideas for involvement
Two-career parents	Put many things in print, e.g., fliers, newsletters, web pages, etc. These parents will read and keep informed. Ask for e-mail addresses and send a monthly or weekly e-mail that updates them on classroom and school activities.
Involved parents	These parents are at school, volunteering their help. The issue here on occasion is over-involvement, with a few parents seemingly wanting to take on administrative roles. Sometimes the boundaries involving student privacy need to be revisited.
Non-working and uninvolved parents	This occurs at both ends of the economic spectrum. Phone banks, in which parents call other parents and tell them about school activities, begin to create a network. Home contacts are very powerful, as are coffee klatches.
Surrogate parents	These are grandparents, foster parents, et al. They often need emotional support. Assign them a mentor, e.g., a counselor or involved parent who touches base with them once a month.
Immigrant parents	Make short videos dubbed in their own language explaining how school works, how to talk to the teacher, what grades mean, what homework means, etc. Have the videos made by a person in your community from that immigrant group. DO NOT MAKE THEM TOO SLICK OR PROFESSIONAL because then they won't be believed.
Parents working two jobs	Color-code the information you send home. White paper is "nice to know." Yellow paper indicates a concern. Red paper means that immediate attention is needed. You can call these parents at work as long as you do not discuss matters at that time; ask them to call you back. Videos to introduce the teacher work well also.
Single parents	Structure activities that make life easier for the parent—activities that include the children or childcare, food (so they don't need to cook), or activities scheduled on weekends or with open time frames rather than specific meeting times. Videos to introduce the teacher also work well here.

(continued on next page)

(continued from previous page)

Subgroups of parents	Ideas for involvement
Parents who are unavailable and students who, in effect, are their own parents	These are parents who are incarcerated, mentally ill, physically ill, addicted, traveling a great deal, or perhaps have been sent back to their native country. Teach students how to be their own parent and provide linkages for the students to other school service agencies. Have the counselor conduct "what if" lunches where pizza is brought in and four or five students in this situation discuss issues.
Parents who are "crazymakers"	There are only a few of these in a building (less than 1%), but they can devour time and sap energy. These are the parents who constantly have a complaint. Each time a solution is reached, there is a new complaint. School personnel need to take their daily rate, divide it by 8 to calculate an hourly rate, and document the cost of personnel time used by one parent. No board of education wants to know that one parent took $60,000 to $70,000 of personnel time for virtually no reason.

In your campus plan, identify specific ways you will target each group. **It is unrealistic to treat parents as one group. The needs and issues are very different.**

Parent-Involvement Ideas

- Phone systems: Let parents and guardians talk to a person. Phone systems at secondary schools in particular often make it very difficult to talk to a real, live human being.

- Have an awards assembly for *parents*.

- Identify clear mechanisms for communicating information. For affluent and most middle-class parents, a website is wonderful. For all parents, videos work. The videos need to be short and focused. For example, how to talk to your teenager, how to find out what is happening at the high school, how to get your child back to school after a suspension, etc.

- Produce a regular newsletter. But it needs to be simple, clear, and to the point—and it must include many icons or visuals so that it can be used whether you're illiterate or an immigrant or extremely busy. These newsletters can be posted outside the building in glass cases and updated weekly. They also can be posted in supermarkets, convenience stores, Laundromats, etc. The National Honor Society could take it on as a service project. Newsletters can be mailed home, a better option than students carrying them home.

- Pay parents to come in and call other parents. Have a list of things to say and set two rules: You may not discuss teachers, and you may not discuss students other than your own children.

- Have gatherings that involve *food*. For example, anyone can come to the school for 50-cent hot dogs.

- If you do parenting classes, don't call them that. Focus on the student: "How to help your child ..." Many parents of teenagers are desperate for good information about teens. Teenagers are typically tight-lipped and, unless you have much opportunity to be around them, as a parent you may not even know what is "normal." Find ways for individuals with lots of exposure to teenagers to share that information with parents and guardians.

- Adopt a plot of land to keep landscaped and clean. One school in a very poor neighborhood did this. Parents took pride in it. (Some even planted and cultivated tomatoes!)

- Divide parents among all the staff members (secretaries included). Each staff member contacts those parents and tells them, "If you have a question you cannot get an answer to, you can always call me."

- Create emotional safety for parents by being respectful of their concerns, openly sharing school activities, clarifying behavioral parameters and expectations of the school, and identifying available opportunities.

- For all activities, organizations, handbooks, etc., use simpler formats for giving the information. Liberally use visuals to appeal to the illiterate, the immigrant, the busy.

Working with Under-Resourced Parents

There are five issues to address, in this order, when working with under-resourced parents.

1. Mutual respect.
2. The use of casual register.
3. The way discipline is used in the household.
4. The way time is viewed.
5. The role of school and education in their lives.

First, for many parents who are struggling with two jobs, a disability, illness, etc., school is not a high priority. In fact, it is often feared and resented. Their own personal experience may not have been positive, and school is alternately viewed as a baby sitter or a necessary evil, as in "If I don't send my child, I'll have to go to court."

Use these kinds of phrases with parents (these are the types of comments they also can use with their own children):

- "Learning this will help your child win more often."
- "The mind is a mental weapon that no one can take from you."
- "If you do this, your child will be smarter and won't be as likely to get cheated or tricked."
- "Learning this will help your child make more money."
- "This information will help keep your child safer."
- "I know you love and care about your child very much or you wouldn't be here" (but don't say this if you don't mean it).

Getting Parents to Come to the School Setting

One of the big difficulties for many schools is simply getting the parents into the school setting (though this isn't essential, as noted elsewhere, it is helpful). Howard Johnson, a researcher at Southern Florida University, has done work on why urban parents come to school. The main reason they usually come is a crisis. What he has found is that rarely do they come to the school for reasons that school people think are important. So the first question that must be asked when trying to get parents to school is: "What's in it for the parents?"

A study done by the U.S. government with Title I schools looked only at schools that were 75% or more low-income. Administrators of the study then identified students within those schools who achieved and students who did not. They developed a questionnaire looking at criteria in and out of school to understand the variables that made a difference in achievement. Interestingly, whether parents actually went to school or attended meetings at school was not a significant factor. What made the biggest difference was whether or not parents provided these three things for their children: **support, insistence, and expectations.**

Some suggestions for getting parents to come to the school

1. Rather than the meeting format, use the museum format. That way parents can come and go when it's convenient for their schedule and their inclination. In other words, the school would be open from 6 to 9 p.m. Parents could come to one room to watch a video or a student performance. These would be repeated every 20 to 30 minutes. Another room could have a formal meeting at a given time. Another room could have board games for the students. Another room could have food.

2. Serve food. Give gift certificates to grocery stores. These tend to be popular. Another favorite is clothesbaskets that have soap, shampoo, perfumes, etc., since food stamps don't always allow those purchases.

3. Encourage the students to come with their parents—for several reasons. First, school buildings tend to be big and confusing to parents. If the children go with them, the children help them find their way around. Second, a baby sitter frequently isn't available. And third, children are natural icebreakers. Parents meet each other through their children.

4. Have classes that benefit parents. For example: how to speak English; how to fill out a job application; how to get a Social Security card; how to make money mowing yards, doing childcare, baking, and repairing small engines. Also, schools can make their computer labs available on Saturdays to teach things like CAD (computer-aided design) and word processing—simple introductory courses that last four to five Saturdays for a couple of hours each.

Alternative approaches

1. Use video. Virtually every home in poverty has a TV and a DVD player, even if it has very little else. Keep the videos under 15 minutes.

2. For all fliers home, use both verbal *and* visual information.

3. Provide simple, how-to activities that parents can do with children.

Tips for Working with Parents Who Are Under-Resourced or Undereducated

- Many adults from poverty didn't have a positive school experience. The greeting of the first staff member they encounter (secretary, aide, administrator, teacher) will either confirm their earlier experience or counter it. Some sort of building procedure and greeting should be agreed upon.

- Always call them by Mr. or Mrs. (unless told otherwise). It's a sign of respect.

- Identify your intent. Intent determines non-verbals. Parents from poverty decide if they like you based largely on your non-verbals. If they don't like you, they won't support you or work with you. For example, if your intent is to win, that will be reflected in your non-verbals. Likewise, if your intent is to understand, that will be reflected as well.

- Use humor (not sarcasm). They particularly look to see if you have a sense of humor about yourself. For example: Can you tell a story about yourself in which you weren't the hero? Can you poke fun at yourself?

- Deliver bad news through a story. If you state the bad news directly (e.g., "Your son was stealing"), it will invite an automatic defense of the child. Instead, say, "Let me tell you a story. Maybe you can help me with the situation." Make sure you use the word story.

- If you're comfortable using casual register, use it. If not, don't use it. If you use it in a phony or unrealistic way, they'll probably think you're making fun of them—or they'll lose respect for you.

- Be human and don't be afraid to indicate you don't have all the answers. As alluded to above, parents from poverty distrust people who are "always heroes of their own stories."

- Offer a cup of coffee. In poverty, coffee is frequently offered as a sign of welcome.

- Use the adult voice. Be understanding but firm. Be open to discussion, but don't change the consequences (unless new information surfaces or a better solution can be found).

- Be personally strong. You aren't respected in generational poverty unless you are personally strong. If you're threatened or have an in-your-face encounter, don't show fear. You don't need to be mean; just don't show fear.

- If they're angry, they may appeal to physical power ("I'm going to beat you up!" or "Can we take this outside?"). To calm them, say, "I know you love and care about your child very much or you wouldn't be here. What can we do that would show we also care?" Another phrase that often works is: "Are you mad at me, or are you just mad?"

- Use videos as a way to provide information and communicate with parents. As pointed out above, virtually every U.S. home in poverty has a TV and DVD player. If possible, make the videos entertaining. They can be in any language, but they should be short (less than 15 minutes).

- As noted in Strategy 3, story structure in generational poverty is episodic and random, and the discourse pattern is circular. Understand that these structures take much longer. Allow enough time during conferences for these structures to be used.

- *Home visits by teachers are the fastest and easiest way to build a huge parent support base quickly.* They also significantly reduce discipline issues. Use Title I money to pay teachers to make phone calls and do home visits before there is a problem. (The payoff from this one simple activity is usually tremendous.)

- Remember, the parents from poverty talked about you in the neighborhood before they came to see you. They often made outrageous comments about what they were going to say and do to you before they went to the school (entertainment is an important part of the culture of poverty). So when they return to the neighborhood, they have to report back. Some comments you may end up hearing will be so outrageous that they should be ignored. They were made because they told people in the neighborhood they were going to do so.

- As you discuss situations with parents, ask yourself what resources are available to these individuals. Some suggestions won't work because the resources simply aren't available.

- In middle class, when a topic is introduced that the individual doesn't want to discuss, the individual simply changes the subject. In generational poverty, individuals often say what they think the other person wants to hear, particularly if that person is in a position of authority.

- Emphasize that there are two sets of rules: one set for school and work, another set for outside of school and work.

- As noted earlier, don't accept behaviors from adults that you don't accept from students.

Tips for Working with Highly Resourced and/or Educated Parents

- Don't use humor—at least initially—when discussing their child or situation. If you do, they'll think you don't care about them or their child.

- One of the hidden rules in affluence is: "It's not OK not to be perfect." So identifying your personal weaknesses will not appeal to them particularly. They want to know that you are very good at what you do. On the other hand, if you don't know something, don't try to bluff your way through. They will usually call your bluff.

- Another hidden rule in affluence is that you aren't respected unless you're able to discriminate by quality or artistic merit. Wealthy parents won't respect you unless you have expertise. If you aren't knowledgeable in a particular area, read the experts or get an expert from the school district to sit in with you for the meeting.

- Don't use circular discourse or casual register. They want to get straight to the point and discuss the issue through formal register. They won't respect you if you waste their time.

- Do use the adult voice with affluent parents. Understand that most of them are skilled negotiators. Clearly establish parameters when discussing issues with them. Affluent parents often believe that they and their children are "exceptional" and don't need to follow or adhere to the "rules" of the organization. Be firm about those boundaries.

- Emphasize issues of safety, legal parameters, and the need for the student to develop coping mechanisms for greater success later in life.

- Understand that a primary motivator for wealthy parents is the financial, social, and academic success of their child. They're very interested in what you'll be able to do to help their child be successful.

- When affluent parents come to school and are upset, they likely will appeal to positional power, financial power, or connections ("I know the school board president" … "I'll call my lawyer" …). They also will attack the issues. Be prepared to articulate the issues, and use experts by name in the discussion.

- Don't be intimidated by the affluent parent. Do understand, regardless of your position, who is standing behind you to support you. If you have little or no support above you, make sure you don't paint yourself into a corner. Some affluent parents will rattle the organizational "cage" in order to get what they want.

- Understand the competitive nature of wealth (especially among those with "new money") and the need to excel. Their children are expected to be the best. There tends to be disrespect for those in the service sector, including public service. However, if their child is happy and doing well, most of them will be very supportive.

Conferencing with Parents

Defensive or Overprotective Parents of Any Class

What is driving the protectiveness/defensiveness?

1. Child is a possession: Defend your own no matter what they do.

2. Child is proof of parenting success: It's not OK not to be perfect.

3. Fear of loss: death, affection, loyalty.

4. Loss of another child: want to protect this child.

5. Change personal experience: "My mother never loved me."

6. Beliefs about parenting: "I just want to love him or her."

7. Emotional need of parent: loneliness, co-dependence, addiction.

Questions to ask

1. What is the very worst thing that could happen if we … ?

2. What is the very best thing that could happen if we … ?

3. What coping strategies could your child learn in order to be more successful?

4. I know you love and care about your children very much. What can we do so that you know we love and care about them too?

5. Is there any evidence that the fear is a reality?

6. How will this request help your child be more successful?

7. At what age will you allow your children to be responsible for their own actions?

Interventions

1. Reframing

2. Using a story

3. Establishing the parameters of school success

4. Using other parents to establish perspective

5. Establishing the parameters of parent interventions at school

Appeals

Among highly resourced or highly educated parents, an appeal to the following can be effective: safety, expertise, legalities, or coping strategies in order to be more successful.

Among undereducated or under-resourced parents, an appeal to caring, winning, being smarter, or not getting cheated can be effective.

A Process for Conferencing with Parents

1. Listen. If needed, ask the parent to repeat the conversation and say this, "I am going to put this in writing, and I want you to read back over it to see if I have gotten the main concerns." If you are the administrator, then state that you will share this with the teacher and begin to work on the issue.

2. Ask the parents if this is something they want you to do something about or if they just want you to listen.

3. Pivot the conversation. Find out what the parent wants. Ask, as noted earlier, "Are you angry at me, or are you just angry?" Or: "If you were queen or king, what would be your ideal solution to this?"

4. Establish the parameters, i.e., the limitations of the situation. (In some cases, you must get back with the parents after you've had a chance to check out the legal ramifications.)

5. Discuss options within those parameters.

6. Identify solutions.

7. Establish a plan. If necessary, put the plan in writing.

Parent/Teacher Conference Form with Student

Student name_____

Date_____ Time_____

Parent name_____

Teacher_____

Purpose of the conference (check as many as apply)

_____ scheduled teacher/parent conference

_____ student achievement issue

_____ parent-initiated

_____ discipline issue

_____ social/emotional issue

What is the desired goal of the conference?

What data will I or the student show the parent? Student work, discipline referrals, student planning documents?

What questions need to be asked? What issues need to be discussed? What follow-up tools and strategies will be identified?

Scenarios for Discussion

Scenario: Andrea

Andrea is a senior in high school. The counselor has come to you with a concern. It is the third six weeks of the first semester and Andrea is failing Algebra II honors. Andrea needs Algebra II to graduate. You call the parent in to look at the possibility of Andrea taking regular Algebra II so that she can get the credit and graduate. Algebra II is not offered as a part of summer school.

Andrea's mother comes in for the conference. She informs you in no uncertain terms that Andrea will not switch to an Algebra II regular class. Andrea is going to go to Texas A&M, all her friends are in that class, and she will not be switching. You explain to the mother that she will not have a diploma if she does not get a credit in Algebra II and that without a diploma she will not be admitted into A&M. The mother indicates that Andrea's grades are not the issue. Andrea's friends are the issue, and she is not going to approve the change.

- **What is driving the parent behavior?**
- **What questions would you ask the parent?**
- **What intervention(s) would you make?**

Scenario: Andy Slocum

Andy is in fourth grade. He is one of the youngest students in his class because he was barely 5 in first grade. You like Andy. Mrs. Slocum, his mother, is always at school. The family is very affluent, and Andy is her only child. The gossip network has it that Mrs. Slocum was married before and had two children and lost them in a custody battle.

Mrs. Slocum comes to you in March and tells you that she wants to retain Andy in the fourth grade. She knows he is gifted, but his grades aren't high enough to be in the program. He has been making A's and B's. She wants him to have all A's. From your observations, Andy is a bright child, he is somewhat immature (in comparison to his classmates), but he is very likable, has a winning personality, and is athletically gifted.

You tell Mrs. Slocum about the research regarding retention. The counselor has a conversation with Andy. You talk to the teacher about Mrs. Slocum's request, and the teacher is appalled. You tell Mrs. Slocum that you will not recommend retention. She tells you she will go to the superintendent if you don't recommend retention.

- **What is driving the parent behavior?**
- **What questions would you ask the parent?**
- **What intervention(s) would you make?**

Scenario: Charles

You have a school that is 95% low-income, and at the fifth-grade level you have instituted a decision-making unit. Charles is in fifth grade, and his mother calls you one day and says the following:

"I heard that school was teaching decision making. My son ain't learnin' it. I want you to tell him that he has got to quit stealing so close to home. He needs to go three or four streets over. I don't know what that boy's problem is. That ain't no kind of decision making. If he can't make better decisions, I'm gonna tell the neighborhood about how your school ain't no good. And why they spendin' all that time on makin' decisions when he still don't know how to add?"

- **What is driving the parent behavior?**
- **What questions would you ask the parent?**
- **What intervention(s) would you make?**

Scenario: Michael

You are heading back to your office after visiting classrooms, and Mrs. Walker comes running in the front door. "What is wrong with Michael?" she asks. Michael is her son who's in third grade.

You say, "I haven't seen Michael this morning."

"Well, he just called and said that there is a problem. I need to talk to him."

Michael is called down to the office. During the conversation with his mother, it becomes apparent that Michael is angry with his teacher. He asked to get a drink of water, and instead went to the pay phone, called his mother, and told her to get up there right now. He's angry with his teacher because she gave an assignment he didn't want to do.

- **What is driving the parent behavior?**
- **What questions would you ask the parent?**
- **What intervention(s) would you make?**

Scenario: Mrs. Smith

Mrs. Smith is a loud, gossiping parent who is active in the Parent/Teacher Organization. She has a son and a daughter. The son receives the focus of her attention. Yesterday Mrs. Smith called you because she is furious with you. She wants to know why you didn't do something about those students who put her fifth-grade son, Sam, in the trashcan at lunch. She tells you that if you don't do something about it, she will send her husband up there to "get you."

You aren't as concerned about that as you are that Mrs. Smith will go to the superintendent again with a badly skewed story.

You are surprised. The aides in the lunchroom are excellent, and you haven't heard anything about anyone being put in a trashcan. You talk to the fifth-grade teachers and the aides. No one heard anything about this, nor did they see anything.

So you call Sam in and talk to him. You ask for details about the incident—when, where, who. The details are very fuzzy: No, it wasn't during lunch, it was in the hall. He couldn't remember the names; they stuffed him in there before he could see them.

You probe some more. Finally, Sam says, "Every night when I go home my mom asks me what bad thing happened at school today. If I say nothing, she tells me I'm lying to her. So I decided to tell her I got put in a trashcan."

You recall incident after incident where Mom "rescues" Sam and threatens to send Dad up to see you if you don't do what she wants.

- **What is driving the parent behavior?**
- **What questions would you ask the parent?**
- **What intervention(s) would you make?**

Scenario: Mr. and Mrs. Deshotels

The second-grade teacher comes to you in January and tells you that Jacque has already had 25 absences this school year. The teacher has called Jacque's mother for an explanation, but the only explanation is that Jacque doesn't feel well. You look at her records for the year before; she had 36 absences in first grade.

You call the home and are unable to make contact. You get an answering machine. Finally, you send a letter, outlining the law about absences and stating your concern. You hear nothing. The next week, Jacque is absent another two days. You send a letter requesting a conference and indicate that if the absences continue without explanation, you will be required to take the next legal step.

You get a phone call from Mr. Deshotels. He cusses at you, tells you he will get a lawyer, etc. You find out from his monologue that he is a long-distance trucker, and you ask him if he knows how many absences his daughter has. He replies belligerently that he does. You say that you think 27 absences without a medical cause for one semester are excessive. Suddenly there is silence at the other end of the phone.

- **What is driving the parent behavior?**
- **What questions would you ask the parent?**
- **What intervention(s) would you make?**

Scenario: Mrs. Brown

Mrs. Brown is a member of a very conservative church, and she comes to see you about a novel that is being used in fourth grade. She is very upset that the school would have this book. The book is about a 12-year-old boy who goes on a hunt for a deer and comes to understand who he is. It's a book about coming of age and finding identity. She explains to you that the book is really not about a hunt, but the deer really represents a female and the book is about the sexual hunt. You tell her that the district has a choice option on books and that her daughter does not need to read the book; another book will be found for her daughter.

Mrs. Brown isn't satisfied and tells you that you don't understand. The book isn't suitable for any fourth-grader, says Mrs. Brown, and she will work long and hard to make sure it isn't read by anyone in fourth grade, adding that it's wrong to have a book like that in the schools. She has talked to her minister about it. Her minister is willing to go to a board meeting with her to protest the use of such inappropriate sexual reading in elementary school.

- **What is driving the parent behavior?**
- **What questions would you ask the parent?**
- **What intervention(s) would you make?**

Schools that are successful have mutual respect for parents and listen to their concerns. School officials and parents don't always agree, but the parents don't see the school as an enemy.

As noted, 99% of parents love their child. Many parents have little exposure to other children and don't know what is "normal" or the consequences of the approaches they're taking with their children. Furthermore, institutions like schools have their own limitations and flaws as well. Many parents are simply working so hard to put a roof over the heads of their children that concentrating on school is simply one more piece in an already difficult day.

Steps to Follow

1. A "one-size-fits-all" approach doesn't work with parents. Not all parents are equally resourced. Approach each parent as an individual who has varying resources and needs.

2. Identify in your campus plan multiple approaches to parent involvement. Involvement doesn't necessarily mean physical presence at school. It means parents knowing about their children and what they are doing.

3. Don't conduct "parenting" workshops. Instead, offer workshops like these:
   - "How to make your child smarter/more successful"
   - "How to get your child/teenager to cooperate with you"
   - "What to expect—and the tools to address it—when your teenager is in high school"

4. Make sure that when parents do come to the school, they are greeted with a smile, and their concerns are genuinely heard.

5. Clarify for parents the guidelines that must be followed by adults for the school to be safe.

6. In most cases don't expect to call the parent and get a solution. Rather, set up a conference so that a solution can be reached together and in person.

7. Understand that some parents don't have the resources to deal with issues surrounding their children. Blaming the parent(s) won't change the situation.

Strategy ⑧

Address Neighborhood Effects and Poverty

Develop community collaboration models

As we move deeper into the 21st century, it is important to develop human capacity (talent and expertise) in adults, which in many ways is the new frontier. How do we develop human capital on a mass scale? And then, how do we measure it?

When the United States was primarily agrarian, human capacity was largely developed by the family and faith-based entities. When we were primarily industrial, human capacity was largely developed on a mass scale by the institution (school, corporation, organization, etc.). **But now that we are a knowledge-based economy, the institution alone cannot carry the load because, in large measure, of the neighborhood effects of the community.** Neighborhood effects have been virtually ignored in legislation, which has focused mostly on the institution.

What Does the Research Say?

The research is extensive. In "Poverty and Potential," David Berliner identifies **six out-of-school factors common among the poor that significantly affect learning opportunities for children:**

- Low birth weight and nongenetic influences
- Inadequate medical, dental, and vision care
- Food insecurity
- Environmental pollutants
- Family relations and family stress
- Neighborhood characteristics

Students spend 1150 waking house a year in school and 4700 waking hours per year with their families and in their neighborhoods.

In the area of neighborhood effects, Berliner also identifies the following:

One's ZIP code, both direct and indirect, both positive and negative, affects student achievement.

- In a Chicago study, neighborhood responsibility and trust were measured, which is referred to as "collective efficacy." Low collective efficacy accounted for 75% of the variation in violence levels, and low efficacy is associated with violent crime. Research indicates that "high collective efficacy" can be very powerful in keeping poor children on track.

- Another Chicago study followed poor African American children no matter where they moved and rated the neighborhoods. Students were assessed on verbal ability and achievement testing. States Berliner: "The results showed that staying in neighborhoods of concentrated poverty has a cumulative and negative effect on verbal achievement independent of a host of other factors."

- Neighborhood effects rival family effects in influencing child development.

- Poor neighborhoods have more environmental pollutants.

- There are two types of mobility: opportunity-driven and poverty-driven. Thirty percent of the United States' poorest children have attended at least three different schools by third grade. Middle-class children have a rate that is one-third lower. According to Berliner, "Transient students have more behavioral problems, and the more they move, the greater the severity of the behavioral problems teachers note." Those who move three or more times between the ages of 4 and 7 are 20% less likely to graduate from high school.

- Violence, drugs, and gangs are part of the reality of high-poverty neighborhoods. Domestic violence is particularly damaging to learning. History and experience tell us when the economy is bad and unemployment rises, children do not do well. Ten to 20% of U.S. families have some form of serious family violence annually. Fifty to 60% of women who receive public benefits have experienced physical abuse by an intimate partner at some point in their adult life (other studies put it as high as 82%). The No. 1 killer of African American women between the ages of 15 and 34 is homicide by a current or former intimate partner. Domestic violence usually makes the parent unavailable to the child emotionally. Many children exposed to violence suffer symptoms that resemble post-traumatic stress disorder. In one study with an elementary-grade cohort,

> An increase in the number of children from families known to have a history of domestic violence shows a statistically significant correlation to a decrease in the math and reading test scores among the students' peers ... [T]he negative effects were primarily driven by troubled boys acting out ... (Berliner, "Poverty and Potential").

Brain Processing and Development

Furthermore, there has been significant research on the impact of brain processing and development in poor neighborhoods. Consider the following:

According to the book *Scarcity,* the stress of daily poverty narrows "bandwidth" by 13 IQ points.

A study at Cornell University between 1997 and 2006 in rural upstate New York with 339 children (52% male, 97% white) in three waves indicated that "... The findings suggest that poverty, over the course of childhood and early adolescence, increases allostatic load, and this dysregulation, in turn, explains some of the subsequent deficits in working memory four years later" (Schamberg, "The Cost of Living in Poverty").

At the University of California-Berkley, students from poverty were tested via a brain scanner alongside students from middle class and given tasks to do. Using EEGs, researchers compared the brains of low-income 9- and 10-year-olds with the brains of wealthy children. Reported Mark Kishiyama, lead researcher:

> It is similar to a pattern that's seen in patients with strokes [who] have had lesions in their prefrontal cortex [which deals with executive function] ... It suggests that in these kids, prefrontal function is reduced or disrupted in some way ... (Toppo, "Study").

A University of Chicago study found "a family's exposure to neighborhood poverty across two consecutive generations reduces child cognitive ability by more than half a standard deviation" (Sharkey & Elwert, "The Legacy of Disadvantage").

What Community Model Do We Use to Address Poverty?

It is a twofold model called Bridges and Getting Ahead.

Bridges Out of Poverty is a set of constructs about poverty that we at aha! Process teach to a community's resourced individuals whose resources tend to be stable. These individuals are running institutions and making most of the legislative/community decisions. Bridges teaches them about the reality of being under-resourced.

While these resourced individuals generally make the "rules" in the community, they often have a limited understanding of the reality of living in poverty. Bridges provides a common language for individuals of all three classes— wealth, middle class, and poverty—to work together to solve the issues without blame.

Getting Ahead in a Just-Gettin'-By World is a 16-week class of 2½ hours each that aha! Process provides to under-resourced individuals, offering them the information that most resourced individuals have. The class is limited to 12 individuals and it is not a *taught* class; rather it is a *facilitated* class. The individuals who take the class are called "investigators." Participants are paid a $25 gift card each time they come to the class.

Most adults in poverty are problem solvers, but how you spend your time determines much of what you know. If you are spending much of your time in survival mode, what you can know is severely limited. Because we operate in a knowledge-based economy, it is imperative to have access to the information required to navigate that environment.

Getting Ahead modules include:

- My Life Now (how you spend your time)
- Theory of Change
- Rich/Poor Gap and Research on Causes of Poverty
- Hidden Rules of Economic Class
- The Importance of Language
- Eleven Resources
- Self-Assessment of Resources
- Community Assessment

- Building Resources
- Personal and Community Plans (personal future story and giving back to the community)

More than 50,000 individuals have completed the Getting Ahead class. Here are just a few of the results:

- Dubuque, Iowa: In one year, among 119 Getting Ahead graduates, unemployment dropped from 51% to 25%, full-time employment doubled, and homelessness decreased from 21% to 7%.

- Rural Colorado: Among 165 Getting Ahead graduates, unemployment dropped from 60% to 42%.

- Youngstown, Ohio: Among 300 Getting Ahead graduates, full-time employment increased from 31% to 76%, and 58% of the graduates pursued postsecondary endeavors.

- Muskogee, Oklahoma: Among nearly 200 Getting Ahead graduates, more than 50% decreased their debt, increased their income, opened a checking or savings account, and/or sought some form of higher education.

- Harford County, Maryland: Within 20 weeks of graduating from Getting Ahead, 88% of participants obtained a job and a checking account, and 63% reduced their use of predatory lending and resolved major legal issues (past or present).

A 2015 study by Elizabeth Wahler, Ph.D., of the Indiana University School of Social Work, found that from beginning to end of the Getting Ahead learning experience there were statistically significant improvements in perceived stress, mental health and well-being, social support, self-efficacy, hope, goal-directed planning and behavior, and poverty-related knowledge.

In schools that have implemented Getting Ahead as part of their parent training program, officials have seen decreased discipline referrals, increased attendance, and greater parent engagement.

In Summary

To significantly decrease poverty and its impact on children, any approach must do at least the following:

- Take a two-generation approach. Issues involving both adults and children must be addressed at the same time.

- Address all four causes of poverty: individual choices, community conditions (including jobs), exploitation (sexism, racism, predators), and government/political systems of laws and regulations (example: cliff effect).

- Educate both under-resourced *and* resourced individuals. If you educate only under-resourced individuals (those from poverty), the resourced will continue to make rules, establish policy, and pass laws based on misunderstandings about poverty.

- Use both a technical and a relational approach. In a 2014 article titled "The Face of Poverty" published in the *Stanford Social Innovation Review,* the author notes that if you utilize only a technical approach (job training, transportation, housing, etc.), then when the money is gone, the neighborhood usually reverts to its old ways of thinking and living. To have lasting change, you also must take a cognitive, relational approach.

- Have a common language to discuss and address the issues.

For more information about addressing poverty as a community, please visit our website: www.ahaprocess.com.

Conclusion

Hope for the Future:
the Incredible Power of
a Wonderful Teacher

If students are under-resourced, does that doom them for life?

Not if they're lucky to have a few good teachers—and many times, it is only one.

Over and over again, as I talk to adults who have made it out of very difficult and under-resourced situations, it is a teacher or educator who was the impetus for it. Teachers are often bridging social capital. They bring new ideas, hope, skills, and understandings.

I feel so fortunate that I can be a teacher. It is a gift that was given to me, and I can give it to others. I am blessed. May you also be blessed in your work.

Appendix A

Study Guide: *Under-Resourced Learners (URL): 8 Strategies to Boost Student Achievement*

This study guide includes optional activities to be used after watching the *Under-Resourced Learners* DVD series. In addition, a PDF of this study guide is available online.

Pre-Reading Activity

1. School as an Assessment Center or School as an Improvement Center

   - Divide the room into two.

   - Give each table a big sheet of paper and markers.

   - Give half the tables this question on a note card: What happens in the place called "school" if it is an assessment center? (Examples: track kids, compliance, teach to the test.)

   - Give the other half of the tables this question on a note card: What happens in the place called "school" if it is an improvement center? (Examples: Formative assessment is emphasized, growth is documented, there's an all-kids-can-learn culture.)

   - Use words or symbols to fill the box labeled "school." Discuss what students who are under-resourced need to have at school or bring with them to school so they leave as more resourced individuals.

   - Post.

   - Share.

   - Begin the conversation about all-student success and resourcing students.

2. Situated-Learning Activity

   a. Have each group fill out the chart below by using the phrases in the box below the chart.

   b. Discuss the completed chart.

	Just plain folks	Student	Practicing individual or apprentice
Reasons with			
Acts on			
Resolve			
Produce			

   Source: Brown, Collins, and Duguid, "Situated Cognition and the Culture of Learning."

Well-defined problems	Situations	Symbols
Laws	Emergent problems and dilemmas	Causal models
Negotiable meaning and socially constructed understanding	Casual stories	Fixed meaning and immutable concepts
Conceptual situations	Negotiable meaning and socially constructed understanding	Ill-defined problems

Strategy 1: Assess Resources to Determine Interventions

1. What does it mean to be under-resourced?

2. What are the nine resources identified in this chapter?

3. Rank the nine resources based on which ones you feel are most important for success in school and work. Explain why.

4. Complete an analysis of the resources you had as a middle school or high school student. Identify what or who helped you to develop resources and how.

5. Brainstorm other ways to assess student resources.

6. Do you plan for interventions based on the strength of resources? Do you use interventions based on the strength of resources? Do we involve the student in the planning for intervention?

7. Select one resource and describe the impact it has on school if it is missing; identify interventions that can be made to increase that resource.

Optional Activity

Discussion and debriefing questions after watching Under-Resourced Learners DVD for Strategy 1

- Why is it beneficial for students to assess their own resources?

- What is the purpose of looking at resource bases?

- What are some examples of support systems? If a student is missing support systems, what are some behaviors a student might exhibit in school?

- Complete the "Steps to Follow" identified at the end of the DVD for a student or group of students.

Strategy 2: Build Relationships of Mutual Respect with Students

1. What are the characteristics of relational learning?

2. Rate your campus on the seven characteristics of relational learning. What are your school's strengths and weaknesses?

3. What are the characteristics of mutual respect?

4. Consider students you have in class or had previously in your classroom. At what stage of the six stages of learning were they when you first met them? How did they behave? What could you have done differently based on your understanding of the six stages of learning?

5. Identify ways to build mutual respect in your classroom and building.

6. Brainstorm activities that students can become involved in outside of school.

7. Describe methods for providing a safe environment.

Optional Activity

Discussion and debriefing questions after watching Under-Resourced Learners DVD for Strategy 2

- Dottie Murdaugh shared a story about a student she had in class. Have you had any similar experiences with students?

- Debrief the vignette involving Maurice with a partner. Do you have a student who would benefit from having a similar conversation? ("What can I do to help you?")

- What are some methods you can use to help deal with students in difficult situations like the one in the fight vignette?

- Develop a buildingwide or campuswide plan to address the "Steps to Follow."

Strategy 3: Teach Formal Register and Story Structure

1. Identify another example for each of the five registers of language.

2. Explain the importance of casual register.

3. Explain the importance of formal register and its impact on student achievement.

4. Describe a situation that you witnessed or were involved in where register of language affected the outcome.

5. List examples of casual register that students use in your building, and translate them to formal register.

6. Identify at least five vocabulary words/terms that are in formal register and are important to understand in your content area/discipline. Develop a plan for teaching these words to students.

Optional Activities

Words that make you cringe:

- Give participants note cards and tell them to list words that make them cringe. (Give them two minutes.) Examples: fart, shut up, hate, chick, etc.

- Ask the question, "What if you didn't have another word for that cringe word?" That is what it's like to have only casual register.

- Identify alternative ways to express this in formal register.

Discussion and debriefing questions after watching Under-Resourced Learners DVD for Strategy 3

- Why do we need language? What is language used for?

- Explain what Dr. Payne meant when she said, "Specificity of language is linked to experience."

- What did you notice happened in the vignette when Dr. Payne approached Oscar in a friendlier style?

Strategy 4: Teach Tools for Negotiating the Abstract Representational World

1. Why is an understanding of the "paper world" imperative for students in order to be successful in the world of school and work?

2. What does the research on situated learning teach us about learning in our schools?

3. Explain what is meant by "The more complex the process an individual is involved in, the more parts of that process need to be at the level of automaticity."

4. What are some examples of mental models you use in your discipline and content areas?

5. Explain why mental models are imperative in helping students learn.

6. Develop a list of question stems you could have students use to write questions.

7. Identify three ways you can modify how you teach to help students learn based on the information in this chapter. Or, based on the information in this chapter, identify three instructional changes you will make that will have a greater impact on student learning.

8. How can you modify your content to make it more readily available for your students?

Optional Activities

Revisit recent learning:

- Have teachers meet in groups based on content area and discuss how they currently have students relearn learning targets/standards that are scored at less than proficient. Have groups share.

- Then have groups brainstorm innovative ways they could engage students in the relearning. Have groups share to learn new ideas.

Discussion and debriefing questions after watching Under-Resourced Learners DVD for Strategy 4

- Explain why people who want to be tailors first must learn how to iron.

- Give an example of mediation including the *what, why,* and *how.*

- How can your school building/campus address content availability?

- Discuss ways that you can immediately implement the "Steps to Follow" in your classroom/building.

Strategy 5: Teach Appropriate Behaviors and Procedures

1. Identify procedures you currently use in the classroom by completing the chart. Highlight three or four areas that could use improvement.

2. Reflect on the voice you use most often in the classroom and your interactions with others.

3. Identify a situation in which you used the child voice; how did it help or hinder your getting what you wanted?

4. Identify a situation in which you used the positive parent voice and a situation in which you used the negative parent voice. Describe the impact.

5. Identify several phrases in the adult voice you can use in your interactions with others.

6. Identify ways to encourage appropriate responses to your interactions with students.

7. Brainstorm a plan for direct-teaching appropriate behaviors and responses.

Optional Activities

What does a safe environment look like?

- Give each table a big sheet of paper.
- Groups divide each paper into three sections.
- Have participants draw "safe" from the perspective of the student.
- Have them draw "safe" from the perspective of the family.
- Have them draw "safe" from the perspective of the community.
- Make sure many different colors of markers are available. Colors will provide another way to express "safe."
- Ask these questions:
  - Do your children come to a safe school?
  - Do parents send their children to a safe school?
  - Does the community support a safe school?

'Box It Up':

- At the beginning of the session, teach the skill of "boxing it up" (reframing).
- Ask participants to write down three issues/distractions/thoughts that they are currently dealing with that will keep them from being engaged learners.
- Give each participant an envelope. Have them address the envelopes to themselves.
- Put the distraction papers in the envelopes.
- Ask the participants if they are willing to put all those things in the box. Tell them they can have them back at lunchtime.
- Have them physically put the envelopes in a box. Put the box on a shelf. Return the envelopes at lunchtime.

Discussion and debriefing questions after watching Under-Resourced Learners DVD for Strategy 5

- Explain what is meant by a "systems approach to discipline." Give examples of how you can develop a systems approach.
- Identify some of the most effective phrases Ruby Payne and Rita Pierson used to demonstrate the adult voice in the vignette.
- Identify some of the effective phrases Dr. Payne and Dr. Pierson used to demonstrate the positive parent voice.
- What is the purpose of using the positive parent voice?

Strategy 6: Use a Six-Step Process

1. What is meant by the "effect-cause-effect" method?
2. Complete a grid for your class list using the grid in the book as a model.
3. After reviewing the curriculum calibration chart, record your thoughts and reactions to the research. Consider how much of your curriculum is on grade level.
4. Review the Marzano chart. Identify which strategies you use frequently in class and which ones you should use more often.
5. What forms of assessment do you currently use and why?
6. How can you use student artifacts to monitor your instruction?
7. Consider a student you currently have in class or have had in class previously. Answer the questions provided and identify several interventions that may be (or may have been) effective with that student.
8. Identify which of the six processes discussed in this chapter are being used effectively in your building. What changes are needed to be more effective? How can you embed the six-step process in your building?

Optional Activity

Discussion and debriefing questions after watching Under-Resourced Learners DVD for Strategy 6

- Explain the difference between assessment and accountability.
- Discuss how using the six-step process can help you:
  - Keep track of students.
  - Increase student achievement.

- Why is it important and beneficial to monitor individual students?
- What are some techniques Dr. Payne recommends for monitoring high-quality instruction?
- Explain what Dr. Payne meant when she said, "Grades don't tell us whether students are learning against standards." Do you agree or disagree? Why?
- Review the "Steps to Follow" with your colleagues. Discuss how they can be applied to your current situation.

Strategy 7: Build Relationships of Mutual Respect with Parents

1. Why is it so important to work with parents?
2. How can you involve support systems to help students be successful?
    a. Identify five suggested strategies that you will use. How will you implement the strategies?
3. Review the chart that identifies subgroups and ideas for involvement. Identify three ways to help meet the needs of all subgroups.
4. What are two new things you learned from this chapter that you will try with parents this year?
5. Review the scenarios. Identify clues that are appropriate indicators of what is driving parent behavior. Identify appropriate questions to ask parents based on parents' identified motivation, then identify appropriate interventions based on this information.

Optional Activity

Discussion and debriefing questions after watching Under-Resourced Learners DVD for Strategy 7

- According to Superintendent Jerry Chabot, how were home visits implemented in his school corporation?
- According to Dr. Payne, why is it important to engage parents in helping create a supportive environment for the school?
- Dr. Payne describes the three main styles of parenting. In your own words, explain the three styles and their approaches to choices, consequences, and parameters.
- What impact do choices, consequences, and parameters have on behavior and achievement?

- Discuss the vignette about Kelly and Darryl. Identify several effective phrases that Kelly, the principal, used to defuse the situation.

- Identify the key points from the "Next Stop: Harvard" vignette. What methods did the parent use, and how did the principal respond?

- Identify various approaches you can use at your campus/building to involve parents.

Strategy 8: Address Neighborhood Effects and Poverty

1. After reading about building community collaboration, explain how parent involvement can boost student success.

2. Identify ways to incorporate these strategies in your own community and school district. Identify the key people who would need to be involved.

Optional Activity

Discussion and debriefing questions after watching Under-Resourced Learners DVD for Strategy 8

- Identify core issues that may make a student unavailable to learn.

- According to Heatherly Conway, what impact has the Collaboration For Kids program had on communities?

- Identify one word or phrase that summarizes the comments Wendell or Marcia shared as they discussed the work taking place in their community with Menominee Indian School District. Explain your choice.

- Explain the importance of people in transitioning out of poverty.

- Agree or disagree with the statement that community sustainability is the most pressing issue in today's society.

Appendix B

Examples of Secondary Interventions
Outlined in Strategy 6

Twelfth-Grade Pre-AP
Reasonable Expectations by Six-Week Periods

First Six Weeks	Second Six Weeks	Third Six Weeks
AMOUNT AND TYPES OF READING 7 outside readings (of literary merit) 7 in-class readings (of literary merit); teacher conference 1 novel—assigned AMOUNT AND TYPES OF WRITING Creative essay—Beowulf Personal essay College prompt AMOUNT AND TYPES OF VOCABULARY Literary terms—10 (in context)	AMOUNT AND TYPES OF READING Novel (assigned or student choice) AMOUNT AND TYPES OF WRITING Characterization: hero, personality Practice of prompts (timed writing) AMOUNT AND TYPES OF VOCABULARY Literary terms—1 (in context)	AMOUNT AND TYPES OF READING Novel (assigned or student choice) AMOUNT AND TYPES OF WRITING AP prompts (impromptu), based on literature Motifs in Macbeth AMOUNT AND TYPES OF VOCABULARY Literary terms—1 (in context)

Fourth Six Weeks	Fifth Six Weeks	Sixth Six Weeks
AMOUNT AND TYPES OF READING Novel (assigned or student choice) AMOUNT AND TYPES OF WRITING Research paper AMOUNT AND TYPES OF VOCABULARY Literary terms—research-related	AMOUNT AND TYPES OF READING Novel (assigned or student choice) AMOUNT AND TYPES OF WRITING Explication of poetry Allegory AP prompts (timed writing) AMOUNT AND TYPES OF VOCABULARY Literary terms	AMOUNT AND TYPES OF READING Comedy and/or short stories Drama AMOUNT AND TYPES OF WRITING Personal AMOUNT AND TYPES OF VOCABULARY Literary terms

Eleventh and Twelfth Grades
Literary Analysis, Character, Setting, Theme—Any of 8 or Combination; Seniors Must Use Conflict

Criteria	1	2	3	4
1. Stays on topic	Rambles from idea to idea	Occasionally drifts Some consistency on topic	Remains on topic Response is consistent	Logical, unified, and coherent manner Remains on topic with logic
2. Organization and structure	Little or no order No transitions No topic sentences	Organization apparent with gaps and flaws Some transitions Some use of topic sentences Has introduction, body, and conclusion	Organization apparent, with some flaws Uses transitions Topic sentences Has developed introduction, body, and conclusion but may be uneven	Clear and effective transitions Topic sentences enhance argument Has well- and evenly developed introduction, body, and conclusion, all of which catch reader's attention
3. Language control	Simple sentences and fragments Major spelling and mechanical problems Minimal word choice	Simple sentences used Errors in mechanics and spelling impede understanding Consistent "being" verbs	Some sentence variation Some errors in mechanics Some "being" verbs	Varied and effective sentence usage Few, if any, grammatical errors Few "being" verbs Rich and varied word choice
4. Support and elaboration	No support No elaboration Minimal word choice Unelaborated points Must satisfy need for character, setting, or theme in elaboration (12th grade must add conflict)	Limited word choice Some commentary, usually brief Elaboration may be 1 fully developed reason May use proof	All reasons elaborated but not fully Two types of elaboration Some proof from text Must satisfy need for character, setting, or theme in elaboration (12th grade must add conflict)	Consistent use of proofs from text Every reason elucidated fully, with varied types of elaboration Satisfies need for character, setting, or theme in elaboration (12th grade must add conflict)

(continued on next page)

Eleventh and Twelfth Grades
Literary Analysis, Character, Setting, Theme—Any of 8 or Combination; Seniors Must Use Conflict
(continued from previous page)

Criteria	1	2	3	4
4. Support and elaboration (continued)	No voice or purpose	Must satisfy need for character, setting, or theme in elaboration (12th grade must add conflict) Attempted voice and purpose	Author's voice and/or purpose is included in elaboration	Author's voice or purpose is argued/refuted persuasively
5. Reason and logic	Logic/reasoning not present	Key points resemble list Little cohesiveness in argument	Elaboration and organizational structure are used to support argument, and all are closely aligned Logic/reasoning pattern is strong	Counter points of view are included and refuted May use If …, then … pattern Reasoning is superior

Eleventh and Twelfth Grades
Technical Analysis/Descriptive Problem Solving (Real-Life Situation)

Criteria	1	2	3	4
1. Stays on topic	Rambles from idea to idea Does not address audience or purpose	Occasionally drifts Some consistency on topic Is clear about audience and purpose	Remains on topic Response is consistent Addresses audience effectively as evidenced by word choice, formality, syntactical structure, etc.	Logical, unified, and coherent manner Remains on topic with logic Consistently addresses audience on appropriate level
2. Organization and structure	Little or no order	Organization includes overview of situation Some analysis or problem solving present but no clear pattern	Organization includes overview, as well as key points of analysis/ problem solving	Clarity of overview and key points Patterns of analysis/problem solving are clear and have impact

(continued on next page)

Eleventh and Twelfth Grades
Technical Analysis/Descriptive Problem Solving (Real-Life Situation)
(continued from previous page)

Criteria	1	2	3	4
2. Organization and structure (continued)	No transitions No topic sentences Organizational pattern for analysis and problem solving not present	Some transitions Some use of topic sentences	Uses transitions Topic sentences are tied to organizational pattern May include recommendations in conclusion	Clear and effective transitions Topic sentences enhance delivery of key points
3. Language control	Simple sentences and fragments Major spelling and mechanical problems Minimal word choice	Simple sentences used Errors in mechanics and spelling impede understanding Consistent "being" verbs	Some sentence variation Some errors in mechanics Some "being" verbs	Varied and effective sentence usage Few, if any, grammatical errors Few "being" verbs Rich and varied word choice
4. Support and elaboration	No support No elaboration Analysis/problem solving not present, but may be restatement of information from text or sources Unelaborated points	Some commentary, usually brief Elaboration may be 1 fully developed reason May use proofs	All points elaborated but not fully Two types of elaboration Some proofs from text Pattern of support is clear but unevenly developed	Consistent use of proofs from text Every point elucidated fully, with varied types of elaboration Support central to argument Pattern of support is clear and sound
5. Reason and logic	Very little logic or reasoning present	Analysis is limited Reasoning based on personal perspective rather than text/data Points/support overgeneralized or off mark	Reasoning/logic is accurate Overall reasoning pattern fits argument Data/text used are directly linked to pattern of analysis/problem solving	Reasoning/logic is complete and accurate May extrapolate on analysis, e.g., If …, then … Reasoning/logic is interwoven with organizational structure and support

Enriched/Gate Seventh-Grade Language Arts

First Six Weeks	Second Six Weeks	Third Six Weeks
Vocabulary—80 words	Vocabulary—80 words	Vocabulary—80 words
TAAS (Texas Assessment of Academic Skills) writing—2 persuasive essays (5 paragraphs minimum)	TAAS writing—2 comparison/contrast essays (5 paragraphs minimum)	TAAS writing—2 how-to essays (5 paragraphs minimum)
Research	Research	Research
Literature/reading (skills listed below—3 full-length selections, selected short stories, non-fiction	Literature/reading (skills listed below)—3 full-length selections selected short stories, non-fiction	Literature/reading (skills listed below)—3 full-length selections, selected short stories, non-fiction
Grammar skills	Grammar skills	Grammar skills
Oral presentations (6 per year)		

Fourth Six Weeks	Fifth Six Weeks	Sixth Six Weeks
Vocabulary—80 words	Vocabulary—80 words	Vocabulary—80 words
TAAS writing—2 descriptive essays (5 paragraphs minimum)	TAAS writing—2 essays reviewing all modes/narratives (5 paragraphs minimum)	Writing—poetry/fantasy
Research	Research	Research
Literature/reading (skills listed below)—3 full-length selections, selected short stories, non-fiction	Literature/reading (skills listed below)—3 full-length selections, selected short stories, non-fiction	Literature/reading (skills listed below)—3 full-length selections, selected short stories, non-fiction
Grammar skills	Grammar skills	Grammar skills

- TAAS writing—must include pre-writing, rough draft, final draft, rubrics, correction sheet.
- Vocabulary—compilation from novels, lists, programs.
- Research—bibliography card for six different types of sources, internal footnotes, quote incorporation (reading-based).
- Literature/reading skills—plot/sequential order, setting, characterization, mood, point of view, theme/main idea, cause/effect, flashback, inference, fact/opinion, summarization, recognition of supporting facts/details, logical conclusion, predicting outcomes (foreshadowing), chart/graph interpretation, figurative language, conflict, symbolism, tone, connotation/denotation, other.

Seventh-Grade Pre-AP Stylistic Elements
Reasonable Expectations by Six-Week Periods

First Six Weeks	Second Six Weeks	Third Six Weeks
AMOUNT AND TYPES OF READING	AMOUNT AND TYPES OF READING	AMOUNT AND TYPES OF READING
Outside reading—1 full-length novel	Outside reading—1 full-length novel	Outside reading—1 full-length novel
Teacher-directed—1 novel at least (100–200 pages)	Teacher-directed—1 novel at least (100–200 pages)	Teacher-directed—1 novel at least (100–200 pages)
Figurative language (simile, metaphor, personification)	Figurative language (simile, metaphor, personification)	Figurative language (simile, metaphor, personification)
Supplemented by short stories, poetry, or non-fiction	Supplemented by short stories, poetry, or non-fiction	Supplemented by short stories, poetry, or non-fiction
Oral presentation—once per 6 weeks	Oral presentation—once per 6 weeks	Oral presentation—once per 6 weeks
Grammar, usage, language—no more than 30% of time spent direct-teaching	Grammar, usage, language—no more than 30% of time spent direct-teaching	Grammar, usage, language—no more than 30% of time spent direct-teaching
AMOUNT AND TYPES OF WRITING	Connotation vs. denotation and point of view	Connotation vs. denotation and point of view
Daily writing	AMOUNT AND TYPES OF WRITING	Personification
1 good piece of TAAS (Texas Assessment of Academic Skills) writing	Daily writing	AMOUNT AND TYPES OF WRITING
Enriched/GATE already do more than regular classes—Science Fair, History Fair—and 1 in English with footnotes, bibliography, etc.	1 good piece of TAAS writing	Daily writing
	1 research paper for the year	1 good piece of TAAS writing
AMOUNT AND TYPES OF VOCABULARY	AMOUNT AND TYPES OF VOCABULARY	1 research paper for the year
Minimum 10 words per week vocabulary workshop from Sadlier-Oxford	Minimum 10 words per week vocabulary workshop from Sadlier-Oxford	1 timed (40 minutes) writing in the AP essay format
		AMOUNT AND TYPES OF VOCABULARY
		Minimum 10 words per week vocabulary workshop from Sadlier-Oxford

Enriched/Gate/Pre-AP
Reasonable Expectations

	Sixth Grade		Seventh Grade		Eighth Grade	
	Enriched	Gate/Pre-AP	Enriched	Gate/Pre-AP	Enriched	Gate/Pre-AP
Vocabulary (per six weeks)	50	60	60	80	60–75	90–120
Writing assignments * (per year)	15	17	6	12	6	10
Number of books (in and out of class per year)	Single paragraphs		Multi-paragraphs		Multi-paragraphs	
	10	12	12	16	18	20
Number of projects (per year)	1	3	2	2	3	4
Research (per year)	Introduction to research		1 research paper	1 major research paper	1 major research paper	1 major research paper
					3 reports	4 small reports
Oral presentations (per year)	1	3	6	6	3	4
	Informal		Informal		Informal	

* The number of writing assignments decreases due to length, complexity of topic, elaboration, emphasis on reasoning and logic, etc.

Enriched/Gate Sixth-Grade Language Arts

First Six Weeks	Second Six Weeks	Third Six Weeks
Vocabulary—50 words (compilation of words from lists, novels, and programs) Writing/grammar—In paragraph construction focus on topic sentence, supporting details, concluding sentence (at least 4 samples). Use mini-lessons, rubrics, and correction sheets to address grammar objectives. Research Literature/reading—minimum of 2 full-length selections, as well as selected short stories and non-fiction. Reading skills	Vocabulary—50 words Writing/grammar—In narrative essay focus on 3-part structure: introduction, body, and conclusion. Use writing process to complete 1 final draft. Use mini-lessons, rubrics, and correction sheets to address grammar objectives. Research Literature/reading	Vocabulary—50 words Writing/grammar—In descriptive essay focus on sensory, spatial order, and specific word choice. Use mini-lessons, rubrics, and correction sheets to address grammar objectives. Research Literature/reading

Fourth Six Weeks	Fifth Six Weeks	Sixth Six Weeks
Vocabulary—50 words Writing/grammar—In how-to essay focus on structure and sequential order. Use writing process to complete final draft. Use mini-lessons, rubrics, and correction sheets to address grammar objectives. Research Literature/reading	Vocabulary—50 words Writing/grammar—In comparison/contrast essay focus on structure and strong support. Use writing process to complete final draft. Use mini-lessons, rubrics, and correction sheets to address grammar objectives. Research Literature/reading	Vocabulary—50 words Writing/grammar—In persuasion essay focus on ways to support: Quote from source, dialogue, anecdote, and survey statistics. Use mini-lessons, rubrics, and correction sheets to address grammar objectives. Research Literature/reading

Research/reference materials—encyclopedia, dictionary, atlas, almanac, reader's guide, periodicals (focus on bibliography and note cards).

Literature/reading skills—plot/sequential order, setting, characterization, mood, point of view, theme/main idea, cause/effect, flashback, inference, fact/opinion, summarization, recognition of supporting facts/details, logical conclusion, predicting outcomes (foreshadowing), chart/graph interpretation, figurative language, conflict, symbolism, tone, connotation/denotation, other.

1st Nine Weeks Test

A scientist studied the reproduction
of human skin cells. The scientist examined
several skin cells using a microscope. The
table below summarizes what she learned.

SKIN CELLS		
CELL	PHASE OF DIVISION	CHARACTERISTICS
1	Anaphase	Chromosome separation
2	Telophase	Cytoplasm division
3	Prophase	Visible chromosomes
4	Metaphase	Chromosomes line up

Use the information in the table above to answer the following questions.

1. What process is taking place in all of the cells?

   A) Cell Division
   B) Fertilization
   C) Cytoplasm Division
   D) Chromosome Separation

2. Which is the correct order of the stages, from first to last, in the cell division of a skin cell?

   A) 3,4,1,2
   B) 1,3,2,4
   C) 1,2,4,3
   D) 2,1,3,4

3. Since the process described in the table produces two new identical cells, <u>before</u> it begins, chromosomes in the cell must_____.

   A) Divide in half
   B) Find a mate
   C) Duplicate
   D) Disintegrate

4. Use the provided ruler to determine the length of this line

       A) 5 millimeters
       B) 5 centimeters
       C) 6 millimeters
       D) 6 centimeters

5. Which of the following elements are essential in all living things?
       A) Carbon, Hydrogen, Nitrogen, Sulfur
       B) Carbon, Hydrogen, Nitrogen, Phosphorus
       C) Carbon, Hydrogen, Oxygen, Nitrogen
       D) Carbon, Oxygen, Nitrogen, Potassium

6. Look at each picture closely. Select the pictures that indicate a living item.

A.

B.

C.

D.

E.

F.

G.

H.

1. A, C, D, G

2. E, F, C, B

3. D, E, C, H

4. E, C, F, G

Refer to this diagram of a plant cell to answer the following questions.

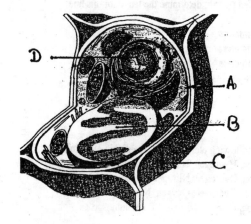

7.. The site of transport of materials into and out of the cell.

   1. A
   2. B
   3. C
   4. D

8. The site of the cell's control center directing all of the cells activities.

   1. A
   2. B
   3. C
   4. D

9. The site that supports and protects the plant cell.

   1. A
   2. B
   3. C
   4. D

10. The site of the cell that stores water, food, waste products and other materials.

   1. A
   2. B
   3. C
   4. D

Source: Developed by teachers at Ridgeroad Middle Charter School, North Little Rock, Arkansas.

DRAFT
8th GRADE MATH
2004-2005

FIRST NINE WEEKS

Basic Operations	1 week
w/Whole Numbers, Fractions & Decimals	
Scientific Notation	
Properties & Exponents	.5 week
Integers/Coordinate Plane	1.5 weeks
Order of Operations	
TEST 1-1	
Equations and Inequalities	2.5 weeks
1 & 2-Step Equations/Inequalities	
TEST 1-2	
Slope	
Rates, Ratio, Proportion, Percent	2 weeks
TEST 1-3	

SECOND NINE WEEKS

Geometry Vocabulary	1.5 weeks
2-D points, Lines, Angles, Polygons	
Geometric Properties and Formulas	2.5 weeks
Triangles, 180°	
Pythagorean Theorem	
Quadrilaterals Properties	
Perimeter/Area	
ll Lines w/Transversals	
TEST 2-1	
Tessellations & Transformations	2 weeks
TEST 2-2	
3-D Geometry	2 weeks
Vocabulary	
Formulas – Surface Area/Volume	
TEST 2-3	

THIRD NINE WEEKS

Data Analysis	.5 week
Mean, Median, Mode, Range	
Construct and Interpret Graphs & Tables	2 weeks
TEST 3-1	
Probability	1 week
Measurement	1 week
TEST 3-2	
Benchmark Preparation	
Algebra	1 week
Geometry	1 week
8th Grade Benchmark	1 week
ALGEBRA A	
Matrices	2 weeks
-Row by Column	
-Adding/Subtracting	
-Scalar Mult.	

FOURTH NINE WEEKS

Slope	1 week
Slope-Intercept Equations	1 week
TEST 4-1	
Function Notation	.5 week
Domain/Range	.5 week
Relations vs. Functions	.5 week
Function Tables	.5 week
TEST 4-2	
Graphing Calculator Activities	**4 weeks**
CBR Activities	
Algebra Project	

Source: Developed by teachers at Ridgeroad Middle Charter School, North Little Rock, Arkansas.

Appendix C

Examples of Elementary Interventions
Outlined in Strategy 6

Missouri Assessment Program Scoring Guide Mathematics	
4 points	**Student's response fully addresses the performance event.** **Response:** ■ Demonstrates knowledge of mathematical concepts and principles needed to complete the event. ■ Communicates all process components that lead to appropriate and systematic solution. ■ May have only minor flaws with no effect on reasonableness of solution.
3 points	**Student's response substantially addresses performance event.** **Response:** ■ Demonstrates knowledge of mathematical concepts and principles needed to complete event. ■ Communicates most process components that lead to appropriate and systematic solution. ■ May have only minor flaws with minimal effect on reasonableness of solution.
2 points	**Student's response partially addresses the performance event.** **Response:** ■ Demonstrates limited knowledge of mathematical concepts and principles needed to complete event. ■ Communicates some process components that lead to appropriate and systematic solution. ■ May have flaws or extraneous information that indicates some lack of understanding or confusion.
1 point	**Student's response minimally addresses performance event.** **Response:** ■ Demonstrates a limited knowledge of mathematical concepts and principles needed to complete the event. ■ Communicates few or no process components that lead to appropriate and systematic solution. ■ May have flaws or extraneous information that indicates lack of understanding or confusion.
0 points	**Student's work consists of copying prompt information only, or the work indicates NO mathematical understanding of task.**

Source: http://www.indep.k12.mo.us/pdc/MAPS/Math8/math_rubric.htm%20copy

First-Grade Reading Benchmarks

First Six Weeks	Second Six Weeks
Writes first name legibly Left-to-right and return sweep (sweep directionality) One-to-one matching Identifies name and main sound for consonant letters Predicts meaning from picture clues	Reads Level 6 book with 90% accuracy, including good fluency Identifies beginning, middle, and end of story (early story structure) Identifies correct sentence structure (begins with capital, ends with punctuation) Identifies beginning and ending sounds of words Identifies differences among letters, words, sentences
Third Six Weeks	**Fourth Six Weeks**
Reads Level 9 book with 90% accuracy, including good fluency Identifies short vowels in words in reading Uses phrasing and punctuation in oral reading	Reads Level 12 book with 90% accuracy, including good fluency Uses self-extending system (*Reading Recovery Guidebook; 7 strategies to use while reading*) Identifies main characters
Fifth Six Weeks	**Sixth Six Weeks**
Reads Level 15 book with 90% accuracy, including good fluency Uses self-extending system Identifies cause and effect in story Retells orally and in writing a story read by teacher and/or independently Identifies story problem	Reads Level 16 book with 90% accuracy, including good fluency Is able to differentiate between non-fiction and fiction Uses self-extending system Chooses appropriate books for independent reading

First-Grade Math Benchmarks

First Semester	Second Semester
Conserves numbers to 8	Writes numbers to 50
More/less	Adds and subtracts numbers without regrouping
One-to-one correspondence	Place value of 1's and 10's
	Addition facts to 10
	Subtraction facts to 10
	Conserves numbers to 10
	Takes steps to decide which operation in (+) or (-) is needed

Reading Rubric, Grade 4

Student name: _____ School year: _____

Campus: _____ Grade: _____

	Beginning	Developing	Capable	Expert
Fluent	Mispronounces common words	Sees word root and endings separately	Understands that prefixes, roots, and suffixes are "changeable parts"	Analyzes pronunciation using analogies to known words and word parts
	Decodes sentences haltingly	Decodes words in context of paragraph	Decoding is non-issue	Reads with expression, fluency, and appropriate tone and pronunciation
Constructive	Can predict what character might do next	Can predict with some accuracy possible endings to story	Can predict more than one ending/solution	Can predict endings to story and explain advantages and disadvantages for author in using various endings
	New vocabulary impairs understanding	Can generate example or synonym for new word	Can generate synonyms, definitions, or antonyms for new word	Uses new vocabulary in writing or speaking
Motivated	Has little understanding of reason for reading	Reads text because teacher said to	Establishes clear purpose for reading	Evaluates purpose for reading
	Has limited interaction with or response to reading	May mention characters read about previously	Compares/ contrasts one piece of reading with/to another	Analyzes personal choices and determines new selections to explore

(continued on next page)

Reading Rubric, Grade 4

(continued from previous page)

	Beginning	Developing	Capable	Expert
Strategic	Does not have enough information to ask questions	Has difficulty asking questions	Can ask questions about what was read	Asks questions that tie together this text and other reading
	Has difficulty differentiating important from unimportant	Can use structure to identify important information	Uses structure to assign order, remember characters, and identify problem/goal	Uses structure to determine most important aspects of text to remember
	Has some difficulty differentiating structure of fiction from non-fiction	Differentiates fiction from non-fiction by structure of piece	Can differentiate among structures used in fiction *	Can differentiate among non-fiction structures **
Process (Before)	Pre-reading strategies involve number of pages and size of print	Identifies purpose for reading	Applies strategies before reading that help better understand what text will be about	Determines strategies needed to better understand selection
(During)	Calls out words and skips words if not understood	Some aspects of text are connected to prior knowledge/experience	Uses some strategies during reading ***	Applies appropriate strategies while reading; can self-correct ****
(After)	Summaries are retelling of as much as is remembered	Can identify favorite part but needs help with summary	Has strategy for categorizing information	Organizes reading by sorting important from unimportant and relating it to purpose and structure

* Fiction structures (examples): Flashbacks, chronological, episodic, story within story.
** Non-fiction structures (examples): Topical, cause and effect, sequential, comparison/contrast, persuasive.
*** Reading strategies: Summarizes and retells events, makes mental picture of what author says, predicts next event, alters predictions based on new information.
**** Self-correction or "fix up" strategies: Looks back, looks ahead, rereads, slows down, asks for help.

Reading Rubric, Grade 5

Student name: _____ School year: _____

Campus: _____ Grade: _____

	Beginning	Developing	Capable	Expert
Fluent	Rate of reading interferes with meaning	Occasionally rate of reading interferes with meaning	Analyzes selection and uses most effective reading rate	Can articulate demands of reading task
Constructive	Has trouble understanding meaning of text	Can understand text but has difficulty formulating questions	Can explain why text is important and can summarize main points	Assigns meaning and relates information in larger context of knowledge
	Vocabulary slows reader	Can use text to make meaning of new vocabulary	Can ask questions about text	Applies vocabulary outside of text and uses it to refine understanding
Motivated	Does not read for information: concentrates on decoding	Holds as much beginning information as possible and forgets rest	Identifies main idea; determines fact and non-fact	Knows specific information needed from text
	Can provide some details about selection	May describe what selection is about and provide some detail	Compares/ contrasts information with/to other events or experiences	Develops questions unanswered by selection
	Reading is initiated by teacher	Reading is initiated by student	Shares reading with others	Actively seeks reading opportunities
Strategic	Differentiates fiction from non-fiction by structure of piece	Can differentiate among structures used in fiction *	Can differentiate among non-fiction structures **	Can articulate and analyze author's use of structure
Sorting	Can remember some of important pieces	Uses structure to assign order, remember characters, and identify problem/goal	Uses structures to determine most important aspects of text to remember	Discusses how structure assists reader in sorting important from unimportant
Asks questions	Does not have enough information to ask questions	Has difficulty asking questions	Can ask questions about what was read	Asks questions that tie this text to others

(continued on next page)

Reading Rubric, Grade 5

(continued from previous page)

	Beginning	Developing	Capable	Expert
Self-correction strategies	Does not self-correct	Recognizes mistakes but has difficulty in self-correcting	Has strategies for self-correction ****	Analyzes self-correction strategies as to best strategy ****
Identifies purpose	Has little understanding of reason for reading	Reads text because teacher said to	Establishes clear purpose for reading	Evaluates purpose for reading
Process **(Before)**	Does not predict	Has some difficulty making predictions	Applies strategies before reading that help better understand what text will be about	Predicts and identifies how author or genre tends to end selections
(During)	Keeps reading if does not understand	Uses some strategies during reading ***	Applies appropriate strategies while reading; can self-correct ****	Analyzes own reading and thinking while reading
(After)	Summaries are retelling of as much as is remembered	Has strategy for categorizing information	After reading, revises schema/conceptual organization	Develops more clarity in thinking as result of reading

*   Fiction structures (examples): Flashbacks, chronological, episodic, story within story.

**   Non-fiction structures (examples): Topical, cause and effect, sequential, comparison/contrast, persuasive.

***   Reading strategies: Summarizes and retells events, makes mental picture of what author says, predicts next event, alters predictions based on new information.

**** Self-correction or "fix up" strategies: Looks back, looks ahead, rereads, slows down, asks for help.

GRADE 1 - FIRST SIX WEEKS - MATH

1. What comes next?

   ◯ △ ▢ ◯ ____

2. What comes next?

   2   4   6   8   ____

3. Circle the odd sets.

4. Circle the even numbers.

   2   4   5   9   8

5.

6. Circle what does not belong.

a   z   f   3

7. Show with tally marks the following numbers.

3 _____   5 _____

8. Draw a line to the box with 4 things.

9. Color the circle blue.
    Color the square red.
    Color the triangle green.

10. How much is there?   _____

Source: Developed with teachers of Runyan Elementary School, Conroe, Texas.

178

Grado 1 – Segundas Seis Semanas – Matematicas

1. ¿Cuántos niños llegan a la escuela en el autobus?

_____

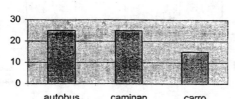

2. Rodea el grupo que tiene menos.

3. Rodea el grupo que tiene menos.

4. Rodea el grupo que tiene más.

5. ¿Cuánto mide el lapiz? _____

6. ¿Cuánto mide el pie del niño? _____

7. Rodea la primera niña.

8. Colorea la séptima pelota.

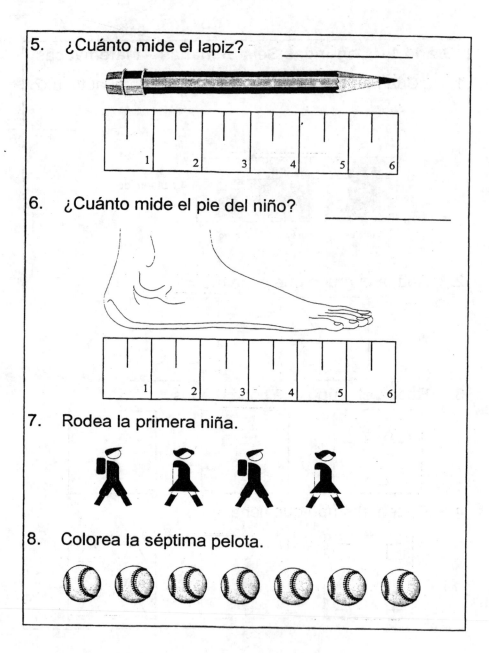

Source: Developed with teachers of Runyan Elementary School, Conroe, Texas.

Appendix D

Strategies for Teacher Training

The following strategies are available to you, the reader, at ahaprocess.com/urlppt as a bonus PowerPoint presentation.

School as an Improvement Center
School as an Assessment Center

1. Answer question #1 or #2.
2. Discuss question and post responses on chart paper.

Question #1

What happens in the place called "school" if it's *an assessment center?*

Question #2

What happens in the place called "school" if it's *an improvement center?*

Overview: Activity 1 Directions (Part 1)

School as an Improvement Center
School as an Assessment Center

1. Complete the *Rate Your Resources Grid*
   (Rubric 1 is low 5 is high)
2. Share your grid responses with your group.

	Financial	Emotional	Mental	Spiritual	Physical	Support Systems	Relationships/ role models	Knowledge of hidden rules	Formal register
1									
2									
3									
4									
5									

Overview: Activity 1 Directions (Part 2)

Concepts Note Cards

1. Write each concept on separate index card #1–6.

- *Relationship of mutual respect (support, insistence, high expectations)*
- *Relational learning*
- *Mental models*

- *Extra learning time*
- *Resource analysis*
- *Technology support in all areas*

2. Order (Prioritize) the note cards to reflect your understanding of the concepts as they relate to your classroom, school, or district.
3. Reorder the note cards. First card ... What we are best at (in our school), to the last card (where we need to add attention and understanding).
4. Select the card with the one concept you will give your full attention to during the workshop and this school year.

Overview: Activity 2

Situated Learning

1. Each group fills in the *Situated Learning Grid* by using the words on the chart.
2. Discuss your completed grid.

	Just plain folks	Student	Practicing individual or apprentice
Reasons with			
Acts on			
Resolve			
Produce			

Well-defined problems	Situations	Symbols
Laws	Emergent problems and dilemmas	Causal models
Negotiable meaning and socially constructed understanding	Causal stories	Fixed meaning and immutable concepts
Conceptual situations	Negotiable meaning and socially constructed understanding	Ill-defined problems

Source: Brown, John Seely, Collins, Allan, and Duguid, Paul. (1989). "Situated Cognition and the Culture of Learning." *Educational Researcher, 18*(1), 32–42.

Overview: Activity 3

Situated Learning Concepts

Well-defined problems	Situations	Symbols
Laws	Emergent problems and dilemmas	Causal models
Negotiable meaning and socially constructed understanding	Causal stories	Fixed meaning and immutable Concepts
Conceptual situations	Negotiable meaning and socially constructed understanding	Ill-defined problems

Overview: Activity 3

Intellectual Capital

1. Write a personal definition of *intellectual capital* on a note card.

2. Share your definition with group.

3. Collaboratively develop a group definition of *intellectual capital* and place on chart paper.

Overview: Activity 4

Remember When

1. Complete the *Rate Your Resources Grid*
   (Rubric 1 is low 5 is high)
2. Share your grid responses with your group.

	Financial	Emotional	Mental	Spiritual	Physical	Support Systems	Relationships/ role models	Knowledge of hidden rules	Formal register
1									
2									
3									
4									
5									

Strategy 1: Activity 1 Directions

Resources Inside and Out

1. Choose one resource from pages 3–13 in the *URL* book.

2. Think about one of your students and answer the yes/no resource questions based on your understanding of that student.

3. Find someone who chose the same resource and compare your responses.

4. Answer the following questions with your partner:
   a. Could you answer the resource questions for your student?
      I. If yes, where did you get that information?
      II. If no, why couldn't you answer the question?
   b. How could you get the information you need about your resource area?
   c. Each resource area share insights.

Strategy 1: Activity 2 Directions

Bonding/Bridging for you and for me

1. Complete the chart by answering the grid questions.
2. Identify who are the people in your bonding and bridging pool.
3. Identify who you are bonding for and whether or not you are bridging for your students.
4. Share with your group.

Bonding: Definition	Who bonded for me?	What did they do for me?
Bridging: Definition	Who bridged for me?	What did they bridge for me?

Bonding	Who do I bond with?	What do I do for them?
	Who did I bridge for?	What am I able to bridge for them?

Strategy 1: Activity 3 Directions

Generalizing Questions

1. **Answer the two generalizing questions with your group.**

   a. Are we using interventions based on the strength of resources and how?

   b. Do we involve the student in the planning for intervention and how?

Strategy 1: Activity 4 Directions

Teacher Then/Teacher Now

1. **Each group will draw a gingerbread man on chart paper. This represents the teacher.**

2. **Group A fills in their gingerbread teacher with descriptors/symbols of *"the teachers then."***

3. **Group B fills in their gingerbread teacher with descriptors/symbols of *"the teachers now."***

4. **Groups will compare and contrast the two drawings and figure out where relational learning fits—*then and now.***

Strategy 2: Activity 1 Directions

Compare/Contrast Verbal Disrespect/Verbal Respect

1. **Individually complete the verbal disrespect /respect grid.**
2. **With a partner role play the *"If ... Then ..."* statements. *If verbal disrespect is… Then verbal respect is….***
3. **Specifically identify what verbal respect sounds like in school.**

If verbal disrespect is:	And sounds like:	Then verbal respect is:	And sounds like:	What's my habit?
Withholding	1. What do I care if you like it? 2. What do you want me to say? 3. I do not have to answer your question			
Countering	1. This assignment is hard. No, it's not; it's easy. 2. You're not fair. Yes, I am.			
Disguised as a joke	1. You couldn't find your head if it wasn't attached. 2. You are so ugly, even your mama couldn't love you.			
Accusing and blaming	1. You are so looking for trouble. 2. You're just trying to pick a fight.			
Judging and criticizing	1. You are lazy. 2. You are stupid. 3. You can't keep anything straight			
Trivializing	1. Next time, do your part. 2. Why did you write your name like that?			

Source: Based on materials from *The Art and Science of Teaching: A Comprehensive Framework for Effective Instruction* by Robert J. Marzano (2007).

Strategy 2: Activity 2 Directions

Find Someone Who

1. Locate the *Find Someone Who* handout and write your name in the free space.
2. Each person needs to have fellow participants sign the spaces of the activity that apply to them. They can only sign if they can give a description of how they do what the square says.
3. You may only sign one square on the game sheet.
4. When the entire sheet is filled, that person yells "Bingo!"

Knows something about each student	Engages in physical behavior that communicates interest	Consistently enforces consequences (positive and negative)
Engages in behaviors that indicate affection	FREE SPACE	Projects a sense of emotional objectivity
Brings student interests into content	Uses humor when appropriate	Maintains a cool exterior

Strategy 2: Activity 3 Directions

Cringe Words

1. Identify and list casual register words that make you **cringe.** Share with a partner.

2. Answer this question, **"What if you didn't have another word for that cringe word?"**

3. What **formal register** words would you substitute for your **"cringe"** words?

Strategy 3: Activity 1 Directions

Language Rich Enviroment

1. Draw two squares on white paper.
2. Brainstorm about what a language rich environment looks like. Fill in the first square with your responses.
3. What can you add to increase the amount of language in your classrooms or schools? Complete the second square based on your specific grade level recommendations.

If we were at our best, what would a language rich environment look like in our schools?	Pick your area: • Elementary School • Middle School • High School

Strategy 3: Activity 2 Directions

Formal/Casual Register Personal Assessment

1. Complete the four-question self-assessment.
2. Share your responses with your group.
3. How does this relate to teaching formal and casual register?

Personal Assessment Questions

1. If three positive comments to one negative comment is the goal, how am I doing with my students?
2. What am I doing to expand my students' knowledge of formal register?
3. Am I respectful of the casual register students bring to our classroom?
4. How do I discipline for poor word choice at school?

Strategy 3: Activity 3 Directions

Reminder to Rock TEACH Formal Register

1. **Take 2 sticky notes and stick them back to back. (or use any tangible item i.e.: a rock)**

2. **Pick a word that is going to remind you to teach formal register.**

3. **Write that word on the sticky note. (write on your tangible item)**

4. **Share the words.**

Strategy 3: Activity 4 Directions

Content Area Abstract Review

1. **Complete the *Abstract Review Grid* based on your area of expertise.**

Content area	What's abstract?	How did I teach it?	How could I teach it?
Administration			
English/ Langauge Arts			
Science			
Math			
Social Studies			
Other			

Strategy 4: Activity 1 Directions

Text Structure Sort

1. **Match the type of organizational structure of text to the Mental Model.**

2. **Text Structure examples:**
   a. **Sequence/how to**
   b. **Story structure**
   c. **Descriptive/topical**
   d. **Persuasive reasoning**
   e. **Compare/contrast advantages/disadvantages cause/effect**

Strategy 4: Activity 2 Directions

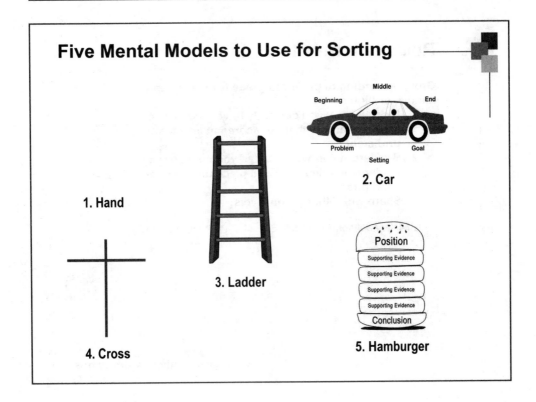

Five Mental Models to Use for Sorting

1. Hand

2. Car

3. Ladder

4. Cross

5. Hamburger

Hint Words: What do they tell us?

1. **Write on paper each of the following words that represent a key to what the text is telling. (*compare/contrast, chronological, description, cause/effect, generalization*).**

2. **Review the word list and place the words in the area that best represents what they are telling.**

usually	furthermore	often
always	additionally	clearly
moreover	because of	conclusively
generally	but also never	effects of
for example	not only	because
in fact	typically	therefore
if … then	in order to	consequently
for this reason	when … then	accordingly
not long after	before	after
afterward	during	following
meanwhile	preceding	then
initially	later	soon
immediately	first	next
when	finally	today
as soon as	now	above
below	across	behind
in front of	in back of	beside
between	over	under
on top of	to the right/left	outside
inside	down	

Strategy 4: Activity 3 Directions

Revisiting New Learning

Group according to preferred grade level: elementary, middle, or high school.

1. **Discuss how you currently have students *relearn* learning targets that are scored at less than proficient.**
2. **Brainstorm innovative ways you *could* engage students in relearning and place the ideas on chart paper.**
3. **Share with other grade levels.**

Elementary School	Middle School	High School

Strategy 4: Activity 4 Directions

What does safe look like?

1. **Groups divide chart paper into three sections and write "safe" in each section.**
   a. In section 1 define *"safe"* from the perspective of the *student.*
   b. In section 2 define *"safe"* from the perspective of the *family.*
   c. In section 3 define *"safe"* from the perspective of the *community.*

Respond to these questions:

1. Do your children come to a safe school?
2. Do parents send their children to a safe school?
3. Does the community support a safe school?

Strategy 5: Activity 1 Directions

Biochemical Issues Read the Research

1. Select an article on *"biochemical issues"* to read and share with your group (jigsaw activity).
2. Read the article and complete the *research guide.*
3. Share your article with your group.

1. Because the research says:
I/we/school/district/grade level need(s) to ...
2. Because the research says:
I/we/school/district/grade level need(s) to ...
3. Because the research says:
I/we/school/district/grade level need(s) to ...
4. Because the research says:
I/we/school/district/grade level need(s) to ...

Strategy 5: Activity 2 Directions

If you choose, then you have chosen ...

1. **Watch the video dealing with resources and resilience from** *Jodi's Stories.*

2. **With a partner role play by using the** *"If you choose, then you've chosen"* **strategy.**
   a. **One** *negative* **response.**
   b. **One** *positive* **response.**

Strategy 5: Activity 3 Directions

Box It Up

1. **List three** *issues/distractions/thoughts* **that you are currently dealing with that may keep you from being engaged learners today.**

2. **Put the list in an envelope and address the envelope to yourself.**

3. **Place your envelopes in the box, you may retrieve them at lunch.**

4. **Discuss distractions that may keep students from learning.**

Strategy 5: Activity 4 Directions

How do they fit?

1. Discuss how can parents and teachers help students to self-regulate and develop the ability to self-govern.

2. Answer the following questions:
    a. Where do I, as the teacher, fit?
    b. Do I understand the parenting styles of my students' parents?

Strategy 7: Activity 1 Directions

Appendix E

Research Findings for Embedding the Strategies in the Long Term

The Payne School Model's Impact on
Student Achievement—A National Study

Dr. William W. Swan, Ed.D., Professor Emeritus, University of Georgia, Educational Leadership Associates

The purpose of this national study was to determine the impact of the Payne School Model (Model) on student achievement in mathematics and English/reading/literacy/language arts in Grades 2, 4–8, and 10. The key elements of the study were:

Research Sites: Five research sites (which were in their first, second, or third year of Model implementation) in school districts in Arkansas, Kansas, New York, Tennessee, and Wisconsin were studied. All sites received technical assistance in implementing the Model.

Time Period: 2003–04 through 2005–06.

Research Design: A quasi-experimental design (Campbell & Stanley, 1963) was used because random assignment was not logistically possible.

Model Fidelity Assessment: The level of Model Fidelity (percentage of the Payne School Model implemented) was determined with teachers at each site.

Student Achievement Tests: Only statewide standardized testing results were used in order to minimize additional testing and avoid interrupting instructional time.

Analyses: The analysis of covariance was used. The independent variable was the High Model Fidelity (50% or more of the Payne School Model) vs. Low Model Fidelity/No Implementation of the Payne School Model. The dependent variables were a student's current-year performance in mathematics and in English/reading/literacy/language arts. The covariate was a student's prior-year performance in mathematics and English/reading/literacy/language arts, respectively.

Sample Sizes: The sample sizes were large. For mathematics, there were 1,176 students in the High Model Fidelity group (experimental) and 2,000 students in the Low Model Fidelity/No Implementation group (comparison). For English/reading/literacy/language arts, there were 851 students in the High Model Fidelity group (experimental), and there were 1,696 students in the Low Model Fidelity/No Implementation group (comparison).

Mathematics (see Table 1 below)

Results for the 20 mathematics analyses are as follows:
- Seven of the results were statistically significant in favor of the High Model Fidelity (HMF) implementation of the Payne School Model.
- Twelve of the results indicated that the Payne School Model was equally as effective as other approaches.
- One result was statistically significant in favor of other approaches.
- Using the normal distribution to determine expected frequencies and analyzing the observed vs. the expected frequencies:
  - There were twice as many positive findings (HMF >) as would be expected in a normal distribution.
  - There were only one-third of the negative findings (HMF <) as would be expected in a normal distribution.
  - Chi-square (with two degrees of freedom) = 6.30, which is statistically significant at the $p < .05$ level.

Table 1: Payne School Model's Impact on Student Achievement in Mathematics: 2004–06

Grade	State(s)/Sites	Sample Sizes			Adjusted Means Differences		
		Exp.	Comp.		HMF > *	HMF =	HMF < *
2nd	TN/1	17	112		1	--	--
4th	KS, TN/2	76	221		--	1	1 *
5th	KS, TN, WI/3	59	364		--	3	--
6th	AR, KS, TN, WI/5	250	624		3 *	2	--
7th	AR, TN/3	337	248		1 *	2	--
8th	AR, NY, TN, WI/5	407	393		1 *	4	--
10th	WI/1	30	35		1*	--	--
	Totals	1,176	2,000		7 *	12	1 *

English/Reading/Literacy/Language Arts (see Table 2 below)

Results for the 19 English/reading/literacy/language arts analyses are as follows:

- Nine of the results were statistically significant in favor of the High Model Fidelity (HMF) implementation of the Payne School Model.
- Nine of the results indicated that the Payne School Model was equally as effective as other approaches.
- One result was statistically significant in favor of other approaches.
- Using the normal distribution for determining expected frequencies and analyzing the observed vs. the expected frequencies:
  - There were three times as many positive results (HMF >) as would be expected in a normal distribution.
  - There were only one-third of the negative findings (HMF <) as would be expected in a normal distribution.
  - Chi-square (with two degrees of freedom) = 14.40, which is statistically significant at the $p < .001$ level.

Table 2: Payne School Model's Impact on Student Achievement in English/Reading/Literacy/Language Arts: 2004–06

Grade	State(s)/Sites	Sample Sizes		Adjusted Means Differences		
		Exp.	Comp.	HMF > *	HMF =	HMF < *
2nd	TN/1	16	111	1 *	--	--
4th	TN/1	16	126	--	1	--
5th	KS, TN, WI/3	57	216	2 *	1	--
6th	KS, TN, WI/4	107	484	1 *	3	--
7th	AR, TN/3	102	283	--	3	--
8th	AR, NY, TN, WI/6	523	441	4 *	1	1 *
10th	WI/1	30	35	1 *	--	--
Totals		**851**	**1696**	**9 ***	**9**	**1 ***

The large number of statistically significant findings for the Payne School Model strongly supports the efficacy of the Model in improving student achievement in mathematics and English/reading/literacy/language arts.

Bibliography and Interviews

Allee, Verna. (1997). *The Knowledge Evolution: Building Organizational Intelligence.* Newton, MA: Butterworth-Heinnemann.

American Psychiatric Association. (2013). *Diagnostic and Statistical Manual of Mental Disorders* (Fifth Edition). (DSM-5-TR). Arlington, VA: American Psychiatric Publishing.

Anderson, John R. (1996). *The Architecture of Cognition.* Mahwah, NJ: Lawrence Erlbaum Associates, Publishers.

Berliner, David C. (1988). Implications of studies of expertise in pedagogy for teacher education and evaluation. Paper presented at Educational Testing Service Invitational Conference on New Directions for Teacher Assessment, New York, NY.

Berliner, David C. (2009). "Poverty and Potential: Out-of-School Factors and School Success." Boulder, CO, and Tempe, AZ: Education and the Public Interest Center & Education Policy Research Unit. Retrieved from http://epicpolicy.org/publication/poverty-and-potential

Berne, Eric. (1996). *Games People Play: The Basic Handbook of Transactional Analysis.* New York, NY: Ballantine Books.

Biemiller, Andrew. (2000). Vocabulary: the missing link between phonics and comprehension. *Perspectives,* Fall, 26–30.

Bloom, Benjamin. (1976). *Human Characteristics and School Learning.* New York, NY: McGraw-Hill Book Company.

Brandt, Ron. (1988). On assessment of teaching: a conversation with Lee Shulman. *Educational Leadership,* November, 42–46.

Bransford, John D., Brown, Ann L., & Cocking, Rodney R. (Eds.). (1999). *How People Learn: Brain, Mind, Experience and School.* Washington, DC: National Academy Press.

Brown, John Seely, Collins, Allan, & Duguid, Paul. (1989). Situated cognition and the culture of learning. *Educational Researcher,* January-February, 18(1), 32–42.

Caine, Renate Nummela, & Caine, Geoffrey. (1991). *Making Connections: Teaching and the Human Brain*. Alexandria, VA: Association for Supervision & Curriculum Development, Publishers.

Caine, Renate Nummela, & Caine, Geoffrey. (1997). *Education on the Edge of Possibility*. Alexandria, VA: Association for Supervision and Curriculum Development.

CharityTracker. (2017). Homepage. Retrieved from http://www.charitytracker.net

Children's Defense Fund. (2014). State of America's children: 2014. Retrieved from http://www.childrensdefense.org/library/state-of-americas-children/2014-soac.pdf

Children's Defense Fund–Minnesota. (2017). Research library. Retrieved from http://www.cdf-mn.org/research-library/

Coles, Robert. (1989). *The Call of Stories: Teaching and the Moral Imagination*. Boston, MA: Houghton Mifflin Company.

Conway, Heatherly Woods. (2006). *Collaboration For Kids: Early-Intervention Tools for Schools and Communities*. Highlands, TX: aha! Process.

Costa, Arthur, & Garmston, Robert. (1986). *The Art of Cognitive Coaching: Supervision for Intelligent Teaching*. Sacramento, CA: California State University Press.

Covey, Stephen R. (1989). *The Seven Habits of Highly Effective People: Powerful Lessons in Personal Change*. New York, NY: Simon & Schuster.

Crowell, Sam. (1989). A new way of thinking: the challenge of the future. *Educational Leadership*. September, 60–64.

Damasio, Antonio R. (1994). *Descartes' Error: Emotion, Reason, and the Human Brain*. New York, NY: G. P. Putnam Sons.

DeSoto, Hernandon. (2000). *The Mystery of Capital*. New York, NY: Basic Books.

DeVol, Philip E., Payne, Ruby K., & Dreussi Smith, Terie. (2006). *Bridges Out of Poverty: Strategies for Professionals and Communities* (Fourth Edition). Highlands, TX: aha! Process.

DeVol, Philip E. (2006). *Getting Ahead in a Just-Gettin'-By World: Building Your Resources for a Better Life*. (Second Edition). Highlands, TX: aha! Process.

Diaconis, Persi, & Mosteller, Frederick (1989). Methods of studying coincidences. *Journal of the American Statistical Association, 84*, 853–861.

The Education Trust. (2017). Home. Retrieved from https://edtrust.org

Edvinsson, Leif, & Malone, Michael S. (1997). *Intellectual Capital: Realizing Your Company's True Value by Finding Its Hidden Brainpower.* New York, NY: HarperCollins Publishers.

Egan, Kieran. (1986). *Teaching as Story Telling.* Chicago, IL: University of Chicago Press.

Egan, Kieran. (1989). Memory, imagination, and learning: connected by story. *Phi Delta Kappan,* February, 455–459.

The El Puente Project. (2004, December). Latino high school youth in Indianapolis: the El Puente Project in retrospect: May 2001–June 2004. Retrieved from https://issuu.com/latinoyouthcollective/docs/puente_project_3_year_report

Evans, G. W., & Schamberg, M. (2008). Childhood poverty, chronic stress, and adult working memory. Proceedings of the National Academy of Sciences of the United States of America, 106(16): 6545–6549. doi: 10.1073/pnas.0811910106

Evans, Patricia. (1992). *The Verbally Abusive Relationship: How to Recognize It and How to Respond.* Cincinnati, OH: Adams Media.

Fassler, David G., & Dumas, Lynne S. (1997). *Help Me, I'm Sad.* New York, NY: Penguin Books.

Feuerstein, Reuven, et al. (1980). *Instrumental Enrichment: An Intervention Program for Cognitive Modifiability.* Glenview, IL: Scott, Foresman & Co.

Fisher, Roger, & Ury, William. (1983). *Getting to YES: Negotiating Agreement Without Giving In.* New York, NY: Penguin Books.

Freire, Paulo. (2000). *Pedagogy of the Oppressed* (30th Anniversary Edition). New York, NY: Continuum International Publishing Group.

Gladwell, Malcolm. (2000). *The Tipping Point: How Little Things Make a Big Difference.* New York, NY: Little, Brown & Company.

Glickman, Carl D. (1990). *Supervision of Instruction: A Developmental Approach* (Second Edition). Boston, MA: Allyn & Bacon.

Goldratt, Eliyahu M. (1990). Theory of Constraints. Great Barrington, MA: Great River Press.

Goleman, Daniel. (1995). *Emotional Intelligence: Why It Can Matter More than IQ.* New York, NY: Bantam Books.

Goleman, Daniel. (2006). *Social Intelligence: The New Science of Human Relationships.* New York, NY: Bantam Books.

Good, Thomas L., & Brophy, Jere E. (1991). *Looking in Classrooms* (Fifth Edition). New York, NY: HarperCollins Publishers.

Greenspan, Stanley I., & Benderly, Beryl L. (1997). *The Growth of the Mind and the Endangered Origins of Intelligence.* Reading, MA: Perseus Books.

Harrison, Lawrence E., & Huntington, Samuel P. (Eds.). (2000). *Culture Matters: How Values Shape Human Progress.* New York, NY: Basic Books.

Hart, Betty, & Risley, Todd R. (1995). *Meaningful Differences in the Everyday Experience of Young American Children.* Baltimore, MD: Paul H. Brookes Publishing Co.

Hock, Dee. (1999). *Birth of the Chaordic Age.* San Francisco, CA: Berrett-Koehler Publishers.

Hollingsworth, John, and Ybarra, Silvia. (2017). Curriculum and instruction. Retrieved from https://dataworks-ed.com/

Howard, Pierce J. (2000). *The Owner's Manual for the Brain* (Second Edition). Austin, TX: Bard Press.

Hunter, Madeline. (1982). *Mastery Teaching.* El Segundo, CA: TIP Publications.

Idol, Lorna, & Jones, B. F. (Eds.). (1991). *Educational Values and Cognitive Instruction: Implications for Reform.* Mahwah, NJ: Lawrence Erlbaum Associates, Publishers.

Jensen, Eric. (1994). *The Learning Brain.* Del Mar, CA: Turning Point Publishing.

Jones, B. F., Pierce, J., & Hunter, B. (1988). Teaching students to construct graphic representations. *Educational Leadership,* 46 (4), 20–25.

Joos, Martin. (1967). *The Styles of the Five Clocks. Language and Cultural Diversity in American Education.* (1972). Abrahams, R. D., & Troike, R. C. (Eds.). Englewood Cliffs, NJ: Prentice Hall.

Jordan, Heather, Mendro, Robert, & Weerasinghe, Dash. (1997). Teacher effects on longitudinal student achievement. Dallas (Texas) Public Schools. Table 3. www.edtrust.org.

Joyce, Bruce, & Weil, Marsha. (1986). *Models of Teaching* (Third Edition). Boston, MA: Allyn & Bacon.

Joyce, Bruce, & Showers, Beverly. (1988). *Student Achievement Through Staff Development.* New York, NY: Longman.

Lave, Jean. (1988). *Cognition in Practice: Mind, Mathematics and Culture in Everyday Life.* Cambridge, England: Cambridge University Press.

Lave, Jean, & Wenger, Etienne. (1991). *Situated Learning: Legitimate Peripheral Participation.* Cambridge, England: Cambridge University Press.

Littlewood, J. E. (1986). *Littlewood's Miscellany.* Cambridge, England: Cambridge University Press.

Marzano, Robert J. (2007). *The Art and Science of Teaching: A Comprehensive Framework for Effective Instruction.* Alexandria, VA: Association for Supervision & Curriculum Development.

Marzano, Robert J., Pickering, Debra J., & Pollock, Jane E. (2001). *Classroom Instruction that Works: Research-based Strategies for Increasing Student Achievement.* Alexandria, VA: Association for Supervision & Curriculum Development.

Marzano, Robert J., & Arredondo, Daisy. (1986). *Tactics for Thinking.* Aurora, CO: Mid Continent Regional Educational Laboratory.

McCarthy, Bernice. (1996). *About Learning.* Barrington, IL: Excel.

McTighe, Jay, & Lyman, Frank T. Jr. (1988). Cueing thinking in the classroom: the promise of theory-embedded tools. *Educational Leadership,* April, 18–24.

Michigan Department of Education. (2015). Collaborating for success—Parent engagement toolkit. Retrieved from http://www.michigan.gov/mde/0,4615,7-140-5233---,00.html

Miller, Scott C. (2007). *Until It's Gone: Ending Poverty in Our Nation, in Our Lifetime.* Highlands, TX: aha! Process.

MPOWR. (2017). Homepage. Retrieved from http://www.mpowr.com

Mullainathan, Sendhil, & Shafir, Eldar. (2013). *Scarcity: Why Having Too Little Means So Much.* New York, NY: Times Books.

O'Dell, Carla, & Grayson, Jackson C. Jr., with Essaides, Nilly. (1998). *If Only We Knew What We Know.* New York, NY: Free Press.

Oshry, Barry. (1995). *Seeing Systems: Unlocking the Mysteries of Organizational Life.* San Francisco, CA: Berrett-Koehler Publishers.

Palincsar, Anne S., & Brown, A. L. (1984). The reciprocal teaching of comprehension-fostering and comprehension-monitoring activities. *Cognition and Instruction,* 1 (2), 117–175.

Payne, Ruby K. (2002). *Understanding Learning: the How, the Why, the What.* Highlands, TX: aha! Process.

Payne, Ruby K. (2005). *A Framework for Understanding Poverty* (Fourth Revised Edition). Highlands, TX: aha! Process.

Payne, Ruby K. (2005). *Learning Structures.* Highlands, TX: aha! Process.

Payne, Ruby K. (2006). *Working with Parents: Building Relationships for Student Success.* Highlands, TX: aha! Process.

Payne, Ruby K. (2007). *Mental Models for English/Language Arts: Grades 6–12.* Highlands, TX: aha! Process.

Payne, R. K. (2013). *A Framework for Understanding Poverty: A Cognitive Approach* (Fifth Revised Edition). Highlands, TX: aha! Process.

Payne, Ruby K., & Krabill, Don L. (2002). *Hidden Rules of Class at Work.* Highlands, TX: aha! Process.

Payne, Ruby K., & Magee, Donna S. (2001). *Meeting Standards & Raising Test Scores—When You Don't Have Much Time or Money.* Highlands, TX: aha! Process.

Porter, Andrew C., & Brophy, Jere. (1988). Synthesis of research on good teaching: insights from the work of the Institute for Research on Teaching. *Educational Leadership,* May, 74–85.

Putnam, Robert D. (2000). *Bowling Alone: The Collapse and Revival of American Community.* New York, NY: Simon & Schuster.

Resnick, Lauren B., & Klopfer, Leopold. (Eds.). (1989). *Toward the Thinking Curriculum: Current Cognitive Research.* Alexandria, VA: Association for Supervision and Curriculum Development, Publishers.

Ridley, Matt. (2000). *Genome: The Autobiography of a Species in 23 Chapters.* New York, NY: HarperCollins Publishers.

Rieber, Robert W. (Ed.). (1997). *The Collected Works of L.S. Vygotsky (Volume 4: The History of the Development of Higher Mental Functions).* New York, NY: Plenum Press.

Rosenholtz, Susan J. (1989). *Teachers' Workplace: The Social Organization of Schools.* New York, NY: Longman.

Sander, William L., & Rivers, Joan C. (1996). Cumulative and residual effects of teachers on future student academic achievement. www.edtrust.org.

Sapolsky, Robert M. (1998). *Why Zebras Don't Get Ulcers.* New York, NY: W. H. Freeman & Co.

Schamberg, Michelle. (2008). "The Cost of Living in Poverty: Long-Term Effects of Allostatic Load on Working Memory." Ithaca, NY: Cornell University. Retrieved from http://ecommons.library.cornell.edu/bitstream/1813/10814/1/Schamberg%20%20Pov%2c%20Load%2c%20Working%20Mem.pdf

Senge, Peter, et al. (2000). *Schools That Learn: A Fifth Discipline Fieldbook for Educators, Parents, and Everyone Who Cares About Education.* New York, NY: Doubleday-Currency.

Senge, Peter, Ross, Richard, Smith, Bryan, Roberts, Charlotte, & Kleiner, Art. (1994). *The Fifth Discipline Fieldbook: Strategies and Tools for Building a Learning Organization.* New York, NY: Doubleday-Currency.

Sharkey, Patrick, & Elwert, Felix. (2011). "The Legacy of Disadvantage: Multigenerational Neighborhood Effects on Cognitive Ability." *American Journal of Sociology, 116,* 1934–1981.

Sharron, Howard, & Coulter, Martha. (1996). *Changing Children's Minds: Feuerstein's Revolution in the Teaching of Intelligence* (Third Edition). Birmingham, England: Imaginative Minds.

Shulman, Lee. (1987). Assessment for teaching: an initiative for the profession. *Phi Delta Kappan,* September, 38–44.

Shulman, Lee. (1988). A union of insufficiencies: strategies for teacher assessment in a period of educational reform. *Educational Leadership,* November, 36–41.

Steiner, Claude. (1994). *Scripts People Live: Transactional Analysis of Life Scripts.* New York, NY: Grove Press.

Stewart, Thomas A. (1997). *Intellectual Capital: The New Wealth of Organizations.* New York, NY: Doubleday-Currency.

Sveiby, Karl Erik. (1997). *The New Organizational Wealth: Managing and Measuring Knowledge-Based Assets.* San Francisco, CA: Berrett-Koehler Publishers.

Toppo, Greg. (2008, December 7). "Study: Poverty Dramatically Affects Children's Brains." *USA Today.*

Tucker, Bethanie H. (2005). *The Journey of Al and Gebra to the Land of Algebra.* Highlands, TX: aha! Process.

Tucker, Bethanie H. (2007). *Reading by Age 5.* Highlands, TX: aha! Process.

UNICEF. (2007). Child poverty in perspective: An overview of child well-being in rich countries. Retrieved from http://www.unicef.org/media/files/ChildPovertyReport.pdf

University of Minnesota, Division of General Pediatrics and Adolescent Health. (2003). Wingspread declaration: A national strategy for improving school connectedness. Retrieved from http://www.pcsb.org/cms/lib8/FL01903687/Centricity/Domain/202/national_strategy.pdf

U.S. Department of Health and Human Services. (2013). Child maltreatment 2012. Retrieved from https://www.acf.hhs.gov/sites/default/files/cb/cm2012.pdf

Wahlberg, Herbert J. (1990). Productive teaching and instruction: assessing the knowledge base. *Phi Delta Kappan,* February, 470–478.

Watson, Bruce, & Knoicek, Richard. (1990). Teaching for conceptual change: confronting children's experience. *Phi Delta Kappan,* May, 680–685.

Wenger, Etienne. (1999). *Communities of Practice: Learning, Meaning, and Identity.* Cambridge, England: Cambridge University Press.

Wiggins, Grant, & McTighe, Jay. (1998). *Understanding by Design.* Alexandria, VA: Association for Supervision & Curriculum Development, Publishers.

Wilson, Edward O. (1998). *Consilience: The Unity of Knowledge.* New York, NY: Alfred A. Knopf.

Wise, Anna. (1995). *The High Performance Mind: Mastering Brainwaves for Insight, Healing, and Creativity.* New York, NY: Tarcher/Putnam.

Wong, Harry K., & Wong, Rosemary Tripi. (1998). *The First Day of School: How to Be an Effective Teacher* (Revised Edition). Mountainview, CA: Harry K. Wong, Publisher.

Zuckerman, Edward L. (2005). *Clinician's Thesaurus: The Guide to Conducting Interviews and Writing Psychological Reports* (Sixth Edition). New York, NY: Guilford Publishing.

Interviews

Interviews with administrators, teachers, students, and consultants were conducted at:

Blackford, Indiana
Fort Wayne, Indiana
Highlands, Texas
Hutchinson, Kansas
North Little Rock, Arkansas

We thank all involved for their vital participation and cooperation.

WE'D LIKE TO HEAR FROM YOU!

Join us on Facebook
www.facebook.com/rubypayne
www.facebook.com/ahaprocess

Twitter
www.twitter.com/ahaprocess
#PovertyChat
#BridgesOutofPoverty

Pinterest
www.pinterest.com/ahaprocess

Subscribe to our YouTube channel
www.youtube.com/ahaprocess

Respond to our blog
www.ahaprocess.com/blog

Download free resources
www.ahaprocess.com

Visit our online store for related titles by Dr. Payne

- *Research-Based Strategies: Narrowing the Achievement Gap for Under-Resourced Learners*
- *How Much of Yourself Do You Own? A Process for Building Your Emotional Resources* (Payne & Baker-O'Neill)
- *From Understanding Poverty to Building Human Capacity: Ruby Payne's Articles on Transforming Individuals, Families, Schools, Churches, and Communities*
- *Working with Students: Discipline Strategies for the Classroom*
- *Removing the Mask: How to Identify and Develop Giftedness in Students from Poverty* (Payne & Slocumb)

Go to www.ahaprocess.com/events for online offerings, including Trainer Certification for Framework and more